Alison,
I look forward
to you leading m
to make it a meaningful
part of the Monmouth University
"fabric". Cheers to the future !! :-)
My Best
S ff.

PRAISE FOR
STUCK IN THE MIDDLE SEAT

"I wish Steve wrote this book twenty years ago before I embarked on my first start-up venture—a great resource full of practical and considered advice for anyone embarking on taking the leap. Having sat in the seat alongside Steve (from the other side of the globe) in one of his current ventures, I can honestly say the guy knows how to have fun and does business the right way—firm, fast, and calculated. True to form, he puts 'About the Author' at the back, trying to make it not about him. But his success is one that all midcareer entrepreneurs would jump at given half the chance. He's giving a fantastic head start in these pages."

—Nathan Omodei, director and CEO, The Leisure Collective International—Australia

"I was introduced to Stephen as my 'mentor' via a program at the Clinton Foundation in Philadelphia, more than ten years ago. Over those years I have found him to be a consistent person in my ear helping me and my management team do better. While the world was telling me how successful I was, he has been there

whispering in my ear, 'This is great and all, but you know you could do better.' Now, thankfully, he's written a book to help cut through the BS. In a world of ego, I think you will find Stephen to be a refreshing pause that will make you, just like he has for me, stop, pause, think, and be honest with yourself.''

—Wil Reynolds, founder, SEER Interactive

"Stuck in the Middle Seat is for those that 'do,' not for those waiting for something divine to happen to them. It gives you a jolt of energy, forces you to be introspective, and challenges you to act. Born out of Steve's own hustle, brilliance, and failures, Stuck in the Middle Seat *is an explosion of 'aha!' moments that will jump-start your entrepreneurial spirit and steer you clear of trip wires along the way, in a no-nonsense business perspective."*

—Gina Montana, wealth advisor

"I'll forever remember a strategy planning map that Steve provided me when setting up my own business that I have passed onto every manager I have had since. Everything with Steve was simple—his questions, his solutions, his advice, his mission, and his goals. Steve's self-belief oozed from every pore, and we share a common disdain for wasting time and lack of focus."

—David Thompson, CEO, Envision Pharma Group, UK

"Having had the opportunity to learn from Stephen through the years as we grew our company from twenty-five to just under two hundred team members, this book left me feeling like I was sitting across the table from Stephen in one of those meetings, soaking in every word of his experiences. This book is an exceptional recount on the depths of Stephen's business knowledge. Stephen does a

fantastic job providing actionable, thought-provoking stories or 'laws' that make you reflect at every turn of the page. The raw advice and lessons learned he shares are what all business leaders need to hear to understand the depths of what being an entrepreneur truly entails."

—Crystal Anderson, president, SEER Interactive (Philadelphia and San Diego)

"I have been fortunate enough to spend a lot of my work life helping entrepreneurs monetize their hard work and sweat equity by selling their business. Right from the start, I was impressed with Steve's ability to hire the right people, help set the short- and long-term strategy, and then let his people execute the vision without micromanaging the team. Steve was practical, passionate, and results-orientated without the huge ego. I ultimately helped Steve and his shareholders sell the business at a premium price. It was a win/win and one of the better and more fun deals I have helped lead."

—Thomas P. O'Connor, investment banker and managing director, BerkeryNoyes, New York City

"Steve's a regular guy with real passion, energy, and confidence to succeed in business and then pass it along. He's always believed in what he was doing, and that confidence translated into a product that his clients truly valued. Since I met him, he was laser focused on what he was building and did not allow himself or his business to get sidetracked. His ideas, untethered passion, and energy are a recipe that should win every time."

—Robert Melillo, JD, managing director, G&M Health

"I have worked with Steve for fifteen years and can honestly say we worked hard, but under his creative entrepreneurial leadership we always had fun and built a company and a culture that was like no other. In our time together even til today, I experienced many of the rules and lessons outlined in this book. It is all true and all accurate and I still draw on much of it as I continue to lead my business."

—Gary McWalters, president, TGaS Advisors (a division of Trinity Life Sciences)

S T U C K

IN
THE

MIDDLE SEAT

THE FIVE PHASES TO BECOMING A
MIDCAREER ENTREPRENEUR

STUCK
IN
THE
MIDDLE SEAT

STEPHEN E. GERARD

ForbesBooks

Published by ForbesBooks, Charleston, South Carolina.
Member of Advantage Media Group.

ForbesBooks is a registered trademark, and the ForbesBooks colophon is a trademark of Forbes Media, LLC.

Printed in the United States of America.

10 9 8 7 6 5 4 3 2 1

ISBN: 978-1-95086-347-1
LCCN: 2020912048

Cover and Layout design by David Taylor.

This custom publication is intended to provide accurate information and the opinions of the author in regard to the subject matter covered. It is sold with the understanding that the publisher, Advantage|ForbesBooks, is not engaged in rendering legal, financial, or professional services of any kind. If legal advice or other expert assistance is required, the reader is advised to seek the services of a competent professional.

 Advantage Media Group is proud to be a part of the Tree Neutral® program. Tree Neutral offsets the number of trees consumed in the production and printing of this book by taking proactive steps such as planting trees in direct proportion to the number of trees used to print books. To learn more about Tree Neutral, please visit **www.treeneutral.com.**

Since 1917, Forbes has remained steadfast in its mission to serve as the defining voice of entrepreneurial capitalism. ForbesBooks, launched in 2016 through a partnership with Advantage Media Group, furthers that aim by helping business and thought leaders bring their stories, passion, and knowledge to the forefront in custom books. Opinions expressed by ForbesBooks authors are their own. To be considered for publication, please visit **www.forbesbooks.com.**

This book is dedicated to my wife, Laurie … she never wavered.

CONTENTS

A STORY ABOUT THE TITLE FOR THE BOOK

In preparing to publish this book, I found myself searching for a better subtitle than *The Five Phases to Becoming a Midcareer Entrepreneur*. While I liked the rubric of five phases, I found that using it as a working title was, quite frankly, boring. Recognizing that I was too close to the project and book to really name it, I reached out to a few colleagues asking for help. I asked them to give my manuscript a read and let me know what they thought, and also provide thoughts on a good title for the book.

A few weeks before the deadline of getting the book title settled, a colleague of mine, Shahir Kassam-Adams, who had recently read the book, took some time to meet with me in Philadelphia. As we sat for coffee, he excitedly told me the story I recount below. As you will see, the story resulted in the title for the book. For context, I have known Shahir for roughly ten years and had the good fortune of buying a company with him in 2014 and selling it for a three-to-four-times return in 2018. In fact, he led an effort to buy my first company (TGaS Advisors) in 2010 and actually backed out of the deal during due diligence. While that was a disappointment and might have had me running for the door in terms of working with him, I knew he was a unique businessperson who was worth staying close to. I have always admired his experiences, his wit, his impatience, and his insights. In helping with the book title, he also did not disappoint me.

The story:

Shahir had reviewed my manuscript the day before he was flying from Philadelphia to Boston for business meetings. As he sat at the Philadelphia airport early that morning, it became clear that the one-hour flight to Boston was going to be delayed and possibly canceled. Being a savvy business traveler, he quickly turned to his iPhone and began to look for other flights to Boston. He mused, in retelling me the story, that he also saw a few other savvy travelers doing the same. It became a race to see who could rebook what were probably already full flights to Boston. It turned out that he and a number of other travelers were able to get on another flight ... and they all hustled to the new gate to board it.

As he boarded the flight, he could see that the other rebooked travelers in front of him were all squeezing into middle seats on the plane, since they had all scrambled to get the last seats. As he told it, many of them were midcareer professionals who were sort of road warrior types ... boarding flights to and from clients and assignments. At that moment, as he recalled, it struck him that the book he had read the day before (my Five Phases) was meant for exactly that professional. It was meant for the midcareer (thirty-five-to-fifty-five-year-old) person who had valuable business skills and experiences and had probably always thought about starting their own business so that they could take control of their life! As he settled into his middle seat, he realized that he had found the title and the target audience for my book.

So thanks to Shahir, and cheers to canceled flights! Once he told me this story, there was no turning back from the appropriateness of the title. I can only hope you are not stuck in a middle seat right now reading this, but if you are ... read on!

PREFACE

Don't fear failure … fear regret!

Inside this book, you'll learn about the five different phases that I believe every successful entrepreneur goes through during his or her climb to the top. The book is organized according to these phases, with each containing multiple chapters, or "laws," which each provide their own lessons learned. I pull many experiences from my own career and life, but I also draw upon the examples and expertise of other wildly successful and business entrepreneurs to make a case.

This book is about starting a business from scratch, like I did when I was forty years old and out of work. Since then, I have built, sold, and bought businesses with revenue and transactions in the hundreds of millions of dollars. I am an owner in a number of global businesses and an investor in others, as well as being an advisor to many entrepreneurs and executives. I have had my fair share of ups and downs, and I outline my background more at the end of the book in the About the Author section. The context for this book is forged by my own personal experiences and the experiences and stories of other entrepreneurs I know. This book also draws from recent experiences and events rather than being tales from the old days.

This book is *not* about scaling up an already-existing business (that book is coming next), nor is it about buying an existing business or franchise, or running a division of a larger company. This book's focus is on having an open canvas on which you have ideas about a business, and you want to understand some basic steps and guardrails for getting going. The book tends to skew toward professional services types of business, such as consulting firms, accounting firms, law firms, engineering/building, marketing agencies, advisory services, and larger B2B-type businesses. Said another way, this book does not really dive deep into businesses that might be classic storefront businesses, franchises, or e-commerce ventures. While I'd like to think there is some good general knowledge and lessons in the book that any entrepreneur can take away, my audience is probably that midcareer professional who wants to start a professional services business.

I am hoping it will also be a good read for people who just enjoy business-oriented books. Being an "entrepreneur" has become very fashionable in the last twenty years, and I imagine this book will either serve to reinforce your desire to be an entrepreneur or perhaps rethink it. Either way, it is meant to be an unvarnished account of what one man (me) thinks you need to do to successfully start a business and make it work during the first few years—especially the first year!

This book is written to be "punchy," and I hope it is a fun read. I'll provide real-world examples of some good and some tough lessons learned with real stories of failure and success. The stories I share are not only mine but also come from successful entrepreneurs I know personally. I also hope the book can act as a reference for you and be something you come back to and reread at times.

The book is written in the manner in which I speak—quick and to the point—but hopefully, it is well thought out. It may also tend to skew toward a sarcastic tone, but please do not let that put you off! I believe that being an entrepreneur has been the greatest business journey of my life, and my entire life changed forever when I decided to do it. Sarcasm is just my way of having some fun, especially during the tough times.

This book is not a vanity project, as there are many, many more successful and articulate entrepreneurs out there than I. My vanity ticket has been punched multiple times via some wonderfully successful businesses, awards, and achievements and the blessings of working with truly great colleagues and collaborators. This book is not a testament to me! In fact, I hate the word "I" because the vast majority of *my* accomplishments were team based and achieved through the work of teams.

Finally, I also write this book out of some selfishness. I am often asked by people who may know of my modest success, "What are the secrets to starting a business?" While flattering, that is not a question one answers over coffee or a beer, while surfing, or on a golf course. Hence the selfishness here is to literally be able to hand someone a book when asked that question. I relish the thought of maybe passing along some lessons learned in a more structured and helpful manner versus a five-minute chat about things. I can only hope this book helps provide some of the tools and some of the courage to go for it.

PHASE I—THE IDEA PHASE: GETTING THE RIGHT IDEA AND THE RIGHT BUSINESS MODEL

Entrepreneurs are driven by the necessity
to invent and the freedom to act.

The Idea Phase is about getting the right concept and idea for your business. It's also about getting an understanding of how the business model (how you make money) will work, and what it will take to make it successful.

This phase cannot be rushed because just about everything that follows, including not starting a business, triggers from the idea. It's like getting married. If you pick the right person, it is a joy. If you pick the wrong person, or you become the wrong person, it sucks!

I'll take you through four laws within this phase and encourage you to progress quickly, but cautiously, through them. While I am not a subscriber to the phrase "You only get one chance to get it right," and instead believe you will adapt and pivot the idea, you will

1

need to come out of this phase confident you have something pretty well defined and something that can get traction!

A note of optimism: This phase is one of the more fun phases in your journey because you have an open book and the proverbial green field, blue ocean, whiteboard (you get it!) to work with your ideas. Whenever I speak with successful entrepreneurs, they typically recount this phase as the happiest of times because they had the power and time to dream. The level of excitement during this phase should be contagious and provide you with a ripple effect for the future phases ... which will be a grind.

So here we go ... strap in, and let's get ideating!

Law 1—The Idea: Do It for Love

If your vision of this is starting a fire, you missed the point! This law is about pouring gasoline on an already existing ember.

"Do what you love, and you never work a day in your life." Every successful entrepreneur and every single book on the topic of "what" to start your business in will recite this quote—and they're right.

The problem for me was that I never *really* knew how to define the "it" (what I loved). I did not know how to get below the surface and cobble through the "mirage" of answers that appeared. I'd spend time making lists of what I loved, thinking about what I loved, but it was like putting your finger on Jell-O. Every time I thought I had it, it moved and remained elusive.

Also, I did not have a framework to find it. In lieu of it, what happens is that you tend to gravitate to popular things of the day for ideas to start the business. As an example, when the internet was just coming of age (late 1990s/early 2000s), I kept thinking about internet businesses I could start. Frankly, in retrospect, I did not even grasp what the internet was, yet I was thinking about internet businesses. I was working backward (outside in, you might say) and going nowhere. For the first fifteen or so years of my career, I was using the hot things of the day as a rubric to get the "idea," versus working forward (inside out) from the basis of what I loved to do.

After some thinking and soul-searching, I came up with three filters you need to harmonize to help you find what you love to do and the resulting business idea:

1. When you are going to be doing *it*, you cannot wait to get started.

2. When you are actually doing *it*, you lose track of time.

3. When someone interrupts you while you are doing *it*, you get angry!

Let's look at these three finding-what-you-love filters, one at a time:

1. WHEN YOU ARE GOING TO BE DOING IT, YOU CANNOT WAIT TO GET STARTED.

What is the thing that, when you see it coming up on your calendar or your to-do list, you cannot wait to get started? Maybe it is an activity, a sport, a discussion topic, a TV show, an event, a hobby … making wine or surfing? What do you clear your calendar or to-do list to make time for? The point of this filter is that you need to reflect on what gets you excited—really excited—no matter what it is. It may be a few things, and that is OK. You have time to whittle them down to the one thing or the right thing.

A quick word on "no matter what it is." You might be asking if this soul-searching is totally open ended and can truly mean anything. I would proffer yes, anything! Even if what you love is something as nuts as watching TV, analyzing stocks, mowing the lawn, organizing your garage, cooking, or working out … you get it. You have to search for those one or two things that you cannot wait to do! Now, maybe you need to filter out things that are a) really not too good for you ("I like drinking vodka, so I will 'drink' vodka for a business"), or b) there is really no way to turn into a business, unless making vodka is something you might be passionate about (and moderate your drinking of). The point is this: Do not let this soul-searching for the idea be constrained right now.

2. WHEN YOU ARE ACTUALLY DOING IT, YOU TOTALLY LOSE TRACK OF TIME.

When was the last time you were totally engulfed in something and said, "Oh, crap, where did the time go"? When is the last time you said, "The heck with it, I'm turning the phone off and taking my watch off?" When is the last time you went to a quiet space (for me, it is the local/university library—where I am writing this book right now!) and just got lost in the work or activity?

Once again, you need to reflect on this filter and see where it takes you. Maybe you need to ask your spouse, your partner, and/or your parents for their observations? You may be too close to what you do and should be open to turn to others for their thoughts and observations. Who better than a parent or relative to provide observations on what you love to do?

3. WHEN SOMEONE INTERRUPTS YOU WHILE YOU ARE DOING IT, YOU GET ANGRY!

These are the times you locked your office door (at home or work) or found someplace in the basement to do the work, and then someone started pestering you. When that happened, you said to yourself, "Why can't they just leave me alone for a few hours?" That angry reaction is a marker for you doing something you love. This is when the phone rang, and you got angry that someone had the audacity to call you! To accentuate this marker, you did not answer the phone call and they kept calling—that's when you blew your top. Argh!

Just to clarify, the interruption has to make you angry because you love doing what is being interrupted, not because you are trying to get it over with and are being slowed down.

For example, if you love doing yard work and get interrupted, and it bothers you because you love doing it, then you have it: it's yard work (landscaping). You might want to start a landscaping business or open a plant nursery or something in that area. If you are angry, though, because you just want to get the yard work over with to move on to something else, then you do not have what you love.

These three filters should provide a useful guide to determine what you love and should then be a starting point for a business venture. Better yet, these filters can be confirmation for what you were going to start the business on anyway. In any case, make sure you are embarking on something you love and that it is authentic to you, because it is going to get difficult!

LESSONS LEARNED

What do I love to do: *Analysis* (numbers, money, business results, plans, forecasts, etc.).

I'm a numbers guy! I love the quiet time of sitting at a desk and playing with numbers and analytics.

I typically work in Excel worksheets and/or large easel paper, sitting at a computer, inputting data, playing with numbers, and drawing conclusions! This might sound truly boring to others (which I can understand), but for me, I love doing it. When I took accounting in high school, I can remember being so amazed by the orderly nature of this new thing called accounting. Hell, I was such a geek that I actually taped up balance sheets and P&L statements over the desk in our house when I was in high school. While my cousin had a Farrah Fawcett poster over his bed, I had balance sheets and P&Ls (oofa!).

But let's follow this through the three filters, OK? When I am thinking about doing analysis, I get a sense of excitement about the challenge of doing it. I can't wait to do it, and sometimes I'll get up at 5:00 a.m. to do it undisturbed. I love to close my office door when I am analyzing interesting things, and I lose track of time and get angry when someone interrupts me. It's that simple—I love to do analysis.[1]

Key takeaway: So it should be no surprise that I majored in accounting in college and had an analytically based career. I then started a business in 2003 based on analysis (benchmarking) and comparing metrics and statistics between companies. While I might have initially thought I loved accounting (versus analysis), it turns out

---

1   By the way, I am acutely aware of how geeky this is and sounds. But, hell, I just love it, and I still do to this day!

accounting was a means to an end. Let someone else do the accounting, and then step aside and let me do the analysis!

Words of caution: Whatever it is you love, you should be pretty darn good at it, or have the ability and desire to get good at it. Trying to run with an idea you have no knowledge about—or worse, are not good at or are naive about—will have you ending in failure. Don't get me wrong; you can learn and accelerate as you go, but you have to have some fundamental knowledge and working proficiency for what you love (or frankly, I'd be asking how/why you thought you loved it if it were new to you).

Beware of hobbies! I really liked making homemade wine in my basement and with friends and family. I had done it for ten or so years and gave some thought to this being my idea for starting a business. The problem is that I sort of sucked at it. The wine I made was marginal at best, and I had no desire to learn more of the science of wine making to take it up a notch. When it came to blending wines and using science (enology) to make better wine, I became totally disinterested. If I had tried to start a wine-making business back then, it would have been a disaster. It was a hobby that I enjoyed, but I did not love it.

Words of hope: If you are a midcareer professional, I would hope that you love what you have been doing! If that is the case, then you have the experiences and leadership qualities to launch into a business that is in your wheelhouse, per se. In being an expert in your profession, having had the chance to be a leader in the field and the business, as I outline in the back of the book under the "Some Thoughts on Midcareer Entrepreneurship" section, you are now ready to leverage the two (learning and leading) and get going.

Law 2—Refining the Idea: Whittling Away at It

Good enough is the enemy of great.

—Jim Collins

If you thought finding what you love was a challenge, then Law 2 is going to hurt. Why? Narrowing an idea or business down to something very focused is hard work. It's hard work because you want to use so many rich words to describe it. You are also so close to it that it's hard to whittle down. And finally, when you are working with the idea/business, it is intuitive to try to be everything to everybody, because you want to gain acceptance from everyone. It's natural. We all want to hear that the idea for the business sounds promising. By whittling it down, you will feel like you are minimizing your chances for success. That's where the trap is! If you keep the idea/business too broad or too vague, you will run the risk of having no differentiated appeal.

The more you narrow and crystallize your business's focus, *the more you will actually broaden your appeal.* This is counterintuitive and can be quite scary because it is built to

> The more you narrow and crystallize your business's focus, *the more you will actually broaden your appeal.*

get you more nos from prospects than you might like. That said, it should also get you more yeses, and probably get them more quickly, which is good. By being very sharp about what your business does and does not do, you'll succeed more quickly. It will also allow you to keep whittling it down to the kernel of what it is about. Lastly, you can also adapt it more quickly because it is simple and focused.

By making something narrow and whittled down, you will invariably get rejections like "That idea is not for me" or "It sounds like a niche." I proffer that those are the reactions you want to hear, and hear quickly. The specificity of your idea will provide people (prospective customers, partners and employees) the ability to react to exactly what you are offering. When you get it right, you will start to hear "That is exactly what I have been looking for" and "That's different from anything else in the market."

Hey, look, even the best ideas will need adjusting, tweaking, and narrowing. But by being specific very quickly, you will get from point A (idea) to point B (business and money) more quickly.

While the time spent whittling will become less and less as you get to the kernel of your business idea, it never really ends. You will always be tweaking and carving it a bit, but whittling time will naturally diminish as you advance if you have it right.

Being a New Jersey native, I remember an interview with Patti Scialfa (E Street Band member and the wife of Bruce Springsteen) in which she talked about Bruce's songwriting process being a case of grabbing an idea and whittling away at it. The concept was that he (and she) would work with ideas and whittle them down until they got to their simplest, most fundamental component. I also recall her saying that they never rushed it. And when they finally got to that whittled-down version, they ran with it. The concept of honing your business idea is no different. Grab the concept and whittle it as quickly as you can until you have something crystal clear.

For my whittling processes, I took a number of business ideas to a handful of trusted and respected colleagues and asked for their open-ended opinions. I was not selling something at that time and made sure they knew I was just researching ideas. So in our meetings, I never expressed objection handling or blind pride in the ideas. To whittle things down, I needed to market test and research ideas by presenting them to people, asking some good open-ended questions, and then *shutting up and listening.*

For me, the act of listening is the figurative knife that does the whittling. Conversely, talking is not whittling. Talking is selling or defending your ideas, and at this stage of the business's birth, you should not be doing either of those. You will have plenty of time to defend and sell once you get going. For now, listen and whittle!

LESSONS LEARNED

The premise for my first true entrepreneurial venture in 2004 was deceptively simple. Although it was not obvious at first, it came in the form of seven simple words, which eventually became our tagline and the foundation for the business:

How do other pharmaceutical companies do "it"?

This first venture was about trying to get pharmaceutical companies to privately share information about their commercial (sales and marketing) operations and use that information to compare them (anonymously) to each other. By providing each participating company with comparisons, we were provided fact-based information to make more informed decisions. It was that simple. If you were working within a pharmaceutical company that was asking that natural seven-word question, we had answers for you.

In a grossly oversimplified way, it is like asking all of your friends and families about their cars and using that feedback to help you pick a car. By benchmarking with others, you make better decisions.

It took us about seven or eight months of whittling (internal meetings, sales calls, soul-searching, consulting advice, et cetera) to get to that tagline. We kept it simple and had whittled it down from a much broader idea. It was easy for clients and prospects to react to, easy to buy it from us, and easy to reject it. *When we whittled it down, we took off.*

We progressed to open every sales call and meeting with those seven simple words. Once we said it, we turned to the prospective clients and said, "Have you ever asked that question before?" We got so confident in this simplistic approach to a basic need (wondering how other companies were doing certain things) that we had the audacity to bet it all in the first minute of every meeting.

If a prospect said, "Yes, I ask that question all the time" or "Wow, I was just in a meeting where someone asked that," we knew we had their attention. Equally, when someone said, "No, I don't care what other companies are doing; I want to be different," we either said we did not need to meet their need, or we turned the phrase back onto them. If someone wants to be different from the crowd, then they are actually obligated to know what the crowd is doing so they can prove they are different. Whether the prospective client's answer was yes or no, we were ready. We were ready because we kept it simple.

It was also a case of whittling down more than the words. We whittled down the business model to be advisory and benchmark based versus consulting. We whittled down the data we were going to capture from thousands of elements to hundreds, and we whittled down the processes and methods in which we were going to work to capture and report the data. We whittled away at the whole business ... constantly.

Key takeaway: Whittling down our original, paragraphs-long, broad-based business idea into seven simple words and a tight operating model made all the difference in the world. By simplifying our message and positioning, we started to broadly appeal to a lot of clients.

Law 3—Describing the Idea: Precision Matters

The simplest things to identify are sometimes the hardest because they were right there in front of you the whole time.

In Law 2, you are working to refine the idea and the business's operations by whittling it down to its base components. You are constantly trying to strip it back, simplify it, and find the kernel of the business in it. In Law 3, you are refining the words that describe it, in as precise a way as possible to effectively communicate it. It's really that simple, yet it is challenging.

This is why I implore you to try to be ruthless in getting it down on paper into a dozen-word statement or sentence. Crystallize your ideas and look for the key words (three or four) that describe it, and then link them together. Be very clear in your own mind what your business is and what it is not!

Precision will take time and multiple iterations, and you should always work to get it to the famed elevator pitch. This is where you have a few floors in a moving elevator to say what it is. If you have trouble doing this, you're probably too close to it and overcomplicating it. That's natural, so ask for help. This is also not a bad time to get some outside help (whether from true consulting/advisory help or respected colleagues), because sometimes you end up so close to the situation that it is really hard to simplify. Just take a look at how I described coming up with the name of this book. I was too close to it and needed outside help!

> Simply put, you have to feel it and believe it.

The last thing I will say on this law is that, simply put, you have to feel it and believe it. It has to feel so natural and uncontrived that you want to lead with it all the time. Said another way, I have been in companies that "come down from on high" after a corporate retreat with a new mission/vision statement, and you are left wondering, "How many martinis did they actually drink get to come up with this crap?" It is not to say they were not well-intentioned company leaders, but more emphasize that it just has to feel natural … where you sort of say, "Of course, that's it!"

While I like to think you do this once and you are done, my experience is that you will be revisiting this often in your first few months and even in the first few years of your business. It could take a few years, as you need to see how your business settles into (or creates) its market with customers and what your team molds it to be. Said another way, expect this to change and adapt fairly frequently in the first year or two, but then expect it to settle in and become pretty stable after that. After a few years (maybe a little longer, depending on the reach and notoriety you achieve in your market), I would argue that you are already in market and probably have established your brand. You have a few short years to perfect this, and then the market owns it.

Here are some examples of what I am getting at in asserting that precision matters:

- Dell: "Yours Is Here."

- Google: "Don't Be Evil." (It was formerly "Search, Ads, and Apps.") This is a good example of how your business's evolution can create a need to advance the precision, even after being in business for years.

- L'Oréal: "Because I'm worth it."

- Microsoft: "Where Do You Want to Go Today?"

- Ford: "Quality Is Job One."

All of the examples above are not only about precision but also about the visceral feeling a brand or product or service can provide. These companies have been at it for years and have the market presence and resources to do this at a whole other level. For your purpose, I would reassert that you are trying to get to a precise description of what you do and what it does for clients.

I will close by using two companies I have an intimate understanding of. Both of these companies have been in business for more than twenty years, and while still relatively small (less than $20 million) by *Fortune* 500 standards, they are meaningful enterprises with lots of employees and hundreds of customers.

1. TGaS Advisors (www.tgas.com; advisory services for pharmaceutical companies):

   TGaS Advisors' benchmarking and advisory services offer *access* to industry experts and a network of professional colleagues, fact-based *answers* to the question "How do other pharmaceutical companies do 'it'?" and practical, actionable *advice* for achieving operational excellence.

   The precision would be something like: "Access … Answers … Advice."

2. The Leisure Collective International (www.creatures.au/; surf equipment and sunglasses):

   In all that we do at Creatures—and we've been doing it for over thirty years now—we strive to meld the lessons of our experience with cutting-edge materials and designs to create highly functional, premium quality surfing accessories that are built to last.

The *precision* would be something like "The Best Surf Accessories on the Planet."

LESSONS LEARNED

When I started the benchmarking company TGaS Advisors, I was relentless on the seven simple words described in Law 2. The reason we existed was to answer: "How do other pharmaceutical companies do it?"

We held the fanatical belief that in *every* pharmaceutical company in the world, in *every* meeting or office, that *every day*, someone was asking those seven simple words. It was our business mantra.

The basis for this lesson learned is to show how those seven simple words had, and did, morph into a better and more precise description of how the business evolved after a few years. After a few years we ended up with fourteen words:

"To be the premier provider of fact-based, trusted advice to the pharmaceutical industry."

The seven simple words then became our tagline and eye-catching phrase that was meant to create pause and interest in *why* we existed. The precise statement above was meant to expand on that by adding and changing a few words. We came in at fourteen words and remained there for roughly six or seven more years ... and then morphed again to:

"TGaS Advisors' benchmarking and advisory services offer *access* to industry experts and a network of professional colleagues, fact-based *answers* to the question 'How do other pharmaceutical companies do "it"?' and practical, actionable *advice* for achieving operational excellence."

While the current "precision" is longer, it advances and captures what the company had become. We also felt that our client base had evolved to include an amazing range of not only long-standing global behemoths in the industry, but also start-up pharmaceutical and biotech companies, and as such, we had a number of new employees who believed the company's remit had grown a bit. Once again, the point of the precision is to describe what you do, whom you do it for, and what the benefits are—in an authentic way. You have to be able to deliver on the promise.

Key takeaway: When you work hard at the whittling (Law 2) and precision (Law 3), you are bound to get it right or close to right, and when you do, it is very empowering. Precision causes you to peel back the reason your company exists and expresses it to all the stakeholders who will matter (customers, partners, employees, and other interested stakeholders). People do not buy what you do, but rather *why* you do it.

Law 4—Adapting It: You Never Get It Right from the Start ... so Adapt It!

Adjust to the conditions, but never the principle.

—Harry Truman

The road to success is always under construction.

The catchword for adapting in this internet era is "pivot," which is actually a good word for this phase. The idea here is that you come to market with an idea/business, but when necessary, you pivot (adapt) that idea so it fits into the vision and market you are either trying to create or compete in. Some pivots can be small tweaks, while others can be profound. Be careful of the profound changes ... here's why.

When you adapt/pivot the idea, make sure Law 1 ("Do what you love") still holds. Is this something you love to do? If it is, keep going! If it differs a lot, then you need to make sure you still want to do it. An easy analogy would be that if you started out to launch a high-end butcher business, but somehow end up becoming a vegetable stand with a few hamburger patties, you had better make sure you are OK with that. You may also realize that what you really loved was providing food (meat, veggies, et cetera) to customers, and it was not really about strictly high-end meats.

I'll provide an analogy closer to home for me. Back in 2004 and 2005, if I needed to pivot my original idea of a *membership-based* benchmark business (clients sign up for one- and two-year memberships) into, let's say, a project-based consulting business, I would have hated it and failed at it! I wanted to develop a complex, information-based business model in which I would work with clients over many years and really get to know them deeply, and thus provide ongoing advice and help. I was not interested in, or good at, one-and-done projects with clients. I had been in consulting models before in which we would do a large, expensive project and move on, and I did not like it at all. It is reinforcement for adapting into something you still love to do.

In fact, I received a lot of advice early on in my first business telling me to go after large consulting projects since we were so close to our clients and had become their advisors. In our benchmarking work, we would often recommend large projects to help our clients advance their capabilities, but we would never do the work. We were implementation agnostic. That meant we were getting the small ($100,000) benchmark contracts and were leaving the large ones ($1 million–$3 million) on the table for others to do. Here is the kernel of the point and a key in adapting: I was happy to leave those large, expensive consulting projects for other firms to do and stick to my benchmarking business. Large consulting projects are unpredictable and unreliable, have long selling cycles, are hypercompetitive, are

> Always consider adapting, but don't ever ditch the core ideals of your business and what you love to do.

scope-changing in nature, are fraught with politics, and have a myriad of other things I don't value or enjoy. Give me the smart, annual advisory contracts all day long that may pale in size to the larger projects but are more predictable, sustainable, and gratifying. To summarize, always consider adapting, but don't ever ditch the core ideals of your business and what you love to do.

Here are some keys to adapting/pivoting when you are still early in the business:

Listen, listen, listen (to prospects and clients … and some outside advisors as well). Listening is the hardest thing to do sometimes. Let's face it: you are proud of your idea, and you're dying to tell people about it. You're dying to get it all out on the table, cutting them off (hopefully politely) when they interrupt with objections. Resist the tendency to defend the idea when it feels like it is coming under attack. Resist the "solve-and-sell" reflex, where you try and answer every objection by trying to force the idea.

Instead, listen to the objections, and ask good, open-ended questions. I personally also like to ask people to numerically rate things (1 being crappy and 10 being unbelievably good) so that it forces them into a definitive position. This also forces me to hear the number, versus me selectively hearing good or bad things. There have been times when I thought I was getting good feedback, asked for a rating, received a 3, and said, "Oh, my, I thought this was good, but it wasn't."

Here are some open-ended questions to ask, and as described, I would ask for a numerical rating to enhance your feedback and potentially advance/pivot your idea:

- How would you rate the idea?

- Would you invest in this if you were a judge on *Shark Tank*?

- Have you seen anyone else try this? Who/which company?

- What works about it? What does not?

- What is the worst thing about this idea?

- Does this compete with anything you are aware of?

- If you could change a few things about it to make it better, what would you do?

- What is the best thing about this idea?

Another good mindset to have in this phase is to stay problem focused (versus solution focused). As long as you can, when you are in the "adapting" mode (which might last for a while), and while you are finding/creating your market, stay focused on the client's business gaps and problems, and continue to ask a lot of questions. You can always design how to fix it, but you only get a few chances to really listen and focus on the problem.

The last thing worth mentioning is to try and get some advice from thoughtful, honest advisors. By taking the time to speak with people on the outside looking in, you will often get a few pearls of wisdom that will help you advance the idea. I have personally found that doing that in a group setting, sometimes at a working breakfast for an hour or so at an off-site location, to be a great use of time and money. By having a few advisors in one place at the same time, you will get them playing off each other's ideas and comments and may end up with even better comments than if you did them one on one.

LESSONS LEARNED

I thought I was doomed at the end of my first year in business ... and it was a good first year! Here's why. Early on in the business, after finishing the first round of benchmarking with some midsize pharmaceutical companies ($500 million to $2 billion in revenue), the dialogue for the next round of benchmarking in the subsequent year went something like this:

TGaS Advisors (me) said, "OK, this was great, and thanks again for the business. We'll be in touch the same time next year. We can come in and redo this benchmark for your company and keep doing it every year. In this way, you will have annual trends and advice!"

Pharma company: "Hey, this was great, but we do not need to do this for another two years because things don't change that much or that quickly. Thanks, and we'll see you around!"

TGaS Advisors' (my) thought: "Oh, crap; this just cut the business in half. We originally thought we would get the same twenty or twenty-five companies to do a benchmark every year, and we'd have a nice, quiet $2 million–$3 million business. Now it looks like we'll only do half that, at best, and none of them want to redo this every year. That means we have zero business going into our second year of business. Talk about one and done!"

As we dealt with the fact that our business model (doing benchmarking every year for our clients) had a fatal flaw in it and were wondering what to do about it, Hurricane Katrina hit the New Orleans area. Right after the hurricane hit, a few of our benchmark clients called us and said, "Hey, can you go ask all those other pharma companies you work with what they think about helping out their sales reps and customers who were affected by the hurricane?"

That was a profound and *adapting* moment for the business!

Our clients essentially took control of our business model, and they took us from being a point-in-time benchmark company to being an ongoing-advice-based company. This was well beyond any once-a-year benchmark business we had imagined. It was in that moment that we realized we were an ongoing, fact-based advisory business, based on gathering relevant and timely facts from the pharmaceutical and biotech industries. It was at that moment that we awakened to a membership model in which clients could join the network for a year or two at time, and we would provide ongoing services to help them make better, fact-based decisions. Wow! All by listening ... and then reacting.

While we started the business with a crisp positioning of a benchmark business, we came to realize after a year or so, that we were a benchmark*ing* business (a continuous business process with ongoing value) versus the occasional benchmark project.

The adaptation: We started out with a *noun* (benchmark) and ended up with a *verb* (benchmarking), and we eventually morphed to being a membership-based advisory business across multiple lines of our clients' departments. And that was good. We listened and adapted and never looked back!

Key takeaway: By actively engaging and listening to smart people (clients, prospects, partners, advisors, and employees), you should be able to adapt your business to be what the market wants and needs. You can do this while remaining true to what you love if you listen and act correctly.

ENTREPRENEURIAL METAL DETECTOR: PROCEED AT YOUR OWN RISK

I wanted to hold off on checkpointing your entrepreneurial journey until you had time with Phase I: the Idea Phase. Allow me a moment for some thoughts on becoming an entrepreneur. Then, the hell with me—forge on to Phase II: the Launch Phase!

While notionally exhilarating, there is nothing easy about starting a business. Even harder is growing that business—hence some well-trodden new business failure statistics:

- Four out of five businesses will fail within five years.

- Only 5 percent of businesses survive ten years.

- Businesses are being disintermediated (put out of business) by new start-ups every day.

In the face of all those metrics on failure, it is still quite fashionable nowadays to be an entrepreneur. Waltzing around the cocktail party talking about your planned venture, posting your plans on Facebook, Instagram, and LinkedIn has never been more in vogue. Who can blame anyone? With all of the legendary stories of the wildly successful entrepreneurs of yesteryear and today, who could resist?

The trouble is that there are not many books about the poor schlubs who were ill prepared, too fast or too slow, tried anyway, and then failed. Those failures don't really make good stories, unless they were able to come back and get it right and win. Those comeback stories are also few and far between. Unwritten are the stories of a) trying and failing and going back to the nine-to-five work world, b) trying and bankrupting yourself (and maybe your family), c) trying and not really knowing how to go about it, and d) trying, succeeding for a brief time, and then going under. Let's not dwell on those failures, but let's recognize they exist … in droves.

So here is a little rubric to sort of calibrate yourself to see if you map to some entrepreneurial traits and characteristics that I have observed in other successful entrepreneurs:

- **Uniqueness.** You don't try to be; you just are. I'm not talking about how you dress here (dressing in Goth clothes or rocking the '80s look), although how you dress and carry yourself are components to this. This is about uniqueness in thinking, in how you process situations and how you approach the world. If you are unique, you should be hearing a lot of "Wow, I never thought of that" or "Hmmm, that's a new way of doing it."

- **Money.** You chase ideas and challenges, not money. Money is important, but it is not the top priority for you. You realize money comes from the best ideas, not vice versa!

- **State of being engulfed.** You just get engulfed in things that interest you and lose track of time and place when you are doing them. Other words for this are *passion* and *focus*. While you may not always be doing the task, you're probably always thinking about it. You'll gladly sit in a dark basement and eat cans of tuna fish to be engulfed by the idea.

- **Speedbumps and setbacks.** You handle them well, quickly, and keep moving forward. You are always able to see the lesson in failures and see the glass as half full. This does not mean you are delusional but more nimble in bouncing back and advancing things.

- **Leadership.** Good, smart people seem to gravitate to you, want to spend time with you, and seek your opinions. Remember, I said *seek* here, versus you always offering your opinion. I also stress *good, smart* people because it is easy to attract dummies and lazy people and have them rely on you.

- **State of being fully present and switched on.** You're always switched on, not in a chaotic way, but it is more that you are always thinking. I had a colleague who called this a brain's rotor speed. You could see this type of person's mind actually spinning in good ways and coming up with unique approaches and thoughts.

> Motivation comes from within, not from your employer.

- **Motivation.** You have evidenced signs of total motivation and focus frequently. Motivation comes from within, not from your employer. As an example, you were the person who went into the office (versus working from home) on the weekends to be able to totally focus and get things done; you were the person who went into the office over a holiday to do the same, or you were the person who woke up at 5:00 a.m. to get after it at your kitchen table. The point of these examples is that you found a place to focus and get things done.

- **Ideas.** You talk constantly about ideas and look for people who make those ideas better. My dad used to repeat the saying, "Great minds talk about ideas, average minds talk about things, and small minds talk about people." Where do you fit?

- **Impatience.** You'd rather die than sit around talking crap. You want to get started on things and figure them out as you go. You like to juggle multiple tasks at once but also have the ability to focus and complete them with some degree of prioritization.

A word of encouragement: Don't despair if you feel you are missing or stretching on some of these traits. Maybe you have some of these traits and should look to partner with another person who brings the traits and skills that you lack. There is nothing wrong with partnering with the right people who can complement your skill set. It will also help decrease the loneliness that is to come.

Finally, in closing out this section, I spoke with a friend and former colleague of mine, David Thompson, who is the CEO of Envision Pharma Group and lives in the United Kingdom. EPG is a sizable company, of which he recently became CEO after starting a business midcareer with another partner after spending seventeen years working for the same company. He has lived the entrepreneurial dream of building and then selling his business to EPG. He has remained on and has risen up to now lead the company. I asked David to describe for me a significant moment or event that he could recall as he was stewing on the idea of striking out on his own, and here is what he told me:

> *The one story I like most, personally, is probably one that precedes my decision to become an entrepreneur. It's the one that most people reading your book may find themselves resonating with most. For me is was about "jumping in" in the first place and leaving a decent, solid job behind. How do you make that decision? I had four kids, college looming, and my wife was a stay-at-home mom. I already had a corner office, seventeen years at the same place, a good career, and a decent amount of security. It's the courage you need to leave and go over the cliff, the top-of-the-roller-coaster, stomach-churner feeling! I did it because my wife said I'd be bitter for years if I didn't, that we could survive month by month for twelve months, and if it didn't work out, I could simply*

go back into a job like my old one, and no one would think negatively of me. By month two, we were onto something. If my wife, Anna, hadn't given me that nudge, I wouldn't have done it. But it's that feeling of "What if?" that you'll always be asking yourself if you don't have the courage to have a go. And is it really failure if it doesn't work out? The failing is in not entering the race and being on that starting line. That's my key lesson.

David's story and "moment" are similar to many stories I have heard over the years—and my own. While not everyone is cut out to be an entrepreneur, many of us are and should give it a go, eyes wide open.

PHASE II—THE LAUNCH PHASE: STARTING THE BUSINESS

Everyone started out as a poor-schlub at some point. This is your poor-schlub phase, so own it, bathe in it, and revel in it.

The Launch Phase is just what it implies—liftoff, hopefully! Up until now, you have kept the rocket grounded, testing your ideas and dialing in what you have with a focus on precision. In the Launch Phase, you're getting out and really testing your ideas and business, trying to find the early believers and the disciples.

While the Idea Phase could not be rushed, in the Launch Phase, it's time to pick up the pace and be all in. No more navel gazing, tuning ideas, and testing the waters. Now it's time to get out and see if you can attract early referrals, buyers, and sponsors. If the Idea Phase was one of the happier times, this phase starts the more nerve-racking times when you will be met with successes and failures.

I'll take you through the two laws within this phase, and I encourage you to move quickly. While you can and will circle back to some adapting and whittling of the business ideas from Phase I, in this phase, you are looking for solid signals of either being on it, pretty close, or way off in terms of what you are offering prospective customers. The scorecard in this phase will be the number of meetings you get, the number of repeat/higher-level meetings you have, and invariably the monetary/contractual commitments you get.

You hopefully will come out of this phase with a concrete business model and some signed contracts/revenue. If you are successful, you will also come out of this phase with a handful of tasty memories that will last a lifetime. For the first handful of sales I made early on in businesses I have been in, I can tell you every twist and turn they took. I can tell you how many meetings I had with each buyer and what made them give me the "go." I can also recount the more than handful of early failures and nos I received. The memories are that vivid.

So here we go … let's launch this thing!

Law 5—Now It Gets Real: Lunching, Selling, and Closing!

Nothing in the world can take the place of persistence. Talent will not—nothing is more common than unsuccessful people with some talent. Genius will not— unrewarded genius is almost a proverb. Education will not—the world is full of highly educated derelicts. Persistence and determination alone are omnipotent.

—Calvin Coolidge

Once you're in the Launch Phase, the business will go through a number of microphases early on. It's important to be aware of each one. The amount of time in each microphase is highly dependent on what type of business you are starting. For me, across a number of start-ups I have been involved in, the Launch Phase took four to six months or so before I was actually up and running and making sales.

THE LUNCHING STAGE

Oh, this is a happy, glorious time. You have an idea that has been fleshed out in the Idea Phase, and now you want to tell and presell it to the world (or your market). It's sort of like the night before Thanksgiving, Christmas, or Hanukkah. Anticipation is high, everything is good, everyone is happy, and tomorrow should be grand. I call this the Lunching Phase because you are doing things in a casual setting. In a casual setting (like over lunch or coffee), you can get a read on good or bad buying signals, possible good next steps, and referrals.

In this initial phase of lunching, you are actually, truth be told, preselling and selling if the opportunity presents itself. Although you may still be refining and adapting your idea/business a little (Law 4), make no bones about it: these encounters, whatever the food or beverages are, are sales calls. During this time, you run around meeting with people you know or are referred to, for lunch or breakfast or dinner, bouncing a pretty firm business model or idea off them and looking for buying signs. The meetings are hopefully with informed, experienced people and folks who can provide referrals and potential customers.

Whereas in the Idea Phase you are testing ideas, now you are testing the desire form someone to buy your service/product. You're really trying to see if they will be a buyer (or maybe referrer). Here are a couple of things you need to get firm answers to during these encounters, because you are probably the one paying for lunch. Consider this your cheat sheet for the conversation:

- Is there a need for the product/service for them, or in their company? You need to be specific here, as you are not looking for general feedback like you did in the Idea Phase. You are looking for a tangible and hopefully urgent or unmet need from them or their company.

- Who/what department will be the buyer and user of the product/service you are selling? Are you with the right person as you eat your Caesar salad, or do they need to refer you to the right person?

- Is there a need right now, at a future time, or ever? Sometimes the timing may be a little off, but the need is there. Alternatively, sometimes there is no need for the product/service.

- Is something filling the need right now? If so, what is it? Is what you are offering different or better?

- What is the price point(s) for what you are selling? Is there an established precedent or range that the person/company is willing to, or has paid in the past?

- Are there any obstacles for people to buy it? What is the process for this person to actually buy your product/service?

Be careful that you have the right person at lunch. Lunching with mental drones, posers, or life suckers (the people who never give back), are typically a waste of time (and your lunch money). Don't get me wrong; it happens a lot. I just want you to be aware of the difference between a genuine prospect and a poser. Also be aware that very few people will be directly honest with you ("Hey, this idea stinks") if your business idea is a bad idea, because it is human nature to not want to kill someone's dreams.

At the end of each encounter, unless a sale has been shut down in advance, ask this: "Would you buy this when I am ready to sell it?" That is when you will get an honest answer. You will also be able to gauge the ability to go back to that person once you are up and running. As I have outlined, make sure the person you are meeting with is the potential buyer/user of your product/service. If they are not, while getting some research with them is good, you have to set up getting to the buyer/user for the next phase, and you need to ask them to help you set up that meeting.

In any case, this is a happy time for most entrepreneurs because you are showing off your ideas and probably having good lunches. After the Lunching Phase, you ideally go back to the Batcave and get onto the next steps identified during that lunch meeting.

THE SELLING STAGE

Now things get a little more serious. In fact, they get a lot more serious. If the Lunching Phase was Christmas or Hanukkah Eve, well, this is Christmas or Hanukkah Morning, and it's time to see if you got the present you were hoping for. Now is when the nerves start to set in … and that's OK.

This phase comes after, or maybe even during, the Lunching Phase, and you have something on the table that someone can say *yes* or *no* to buying or advancing. Here are some things to consider:

- **Sequencing sales calls is important.** When you start the selling stage, go to the least likely one to three prospects first from the Lunching Phase. Why? You need some practice and dry runs for your sales pitch and should burn through your least likely prospects first. Save the whales/best buyers for when you have taken a few trial runs.

- **Make sure you have the absolute right buyer.** This sounds obvious, but if someone is saying yes to buying your product or service, you need to know a) that can they say yes to it, and b) whether there are any other steps to getting a deal. I have had times where I was so excited by a yes that I failed to realize it was a yes to "next steps" … not a yes to buying. Argh! Sometimes you might need a series of yeses to actually get the deal done.

- **Provide options and reasons to say yes in a sales call!** Let me be candid. You have no idea how the market is going to buy, consume, or shape your offering. You may think you do, but you probably do not. That is why I love going to clients/customers with multiple options on how they can buy and engage with what we are offering. First, it is just smart business to give people a range of options to choose from. Second, it gives them a feeling of power in that they get to choose the path forward (it's not one size fits all). Lastly, seeing what options resonate with people help to further shape and adapt the idea by seeing what they gravitate toward. Never go in with one option or all-or-nothing sales propositions if you can avoid it.

- **Provide special offers.** Think about a special offer (without sounding gimmicky). Maybe you want to do a soft launch with a few people. Maybe there is a charter group that would sign up, knowing that they are early adopters, and with that, they receive certain unique benefits. Maybe there is a money-back guarantee ("Hey, pay me at the end if you feel this delivered what we promised!"). For me, a money-back guarantee (or frankly, "Don't pay me until we are done") is a way of me putting our money where our mouth is. It is not a mechanism to look cheap or unsure. It is, in fact, the opposite, because you are so sure you will exceed expectations that you are willing to bet on it. The point of special offers is that you can be flexible, and you can use that flexibility to show confidence in what you are doing.

- **Be crisp in the sales meeting.** Give people something to say yes or no to. Said another way, being too vague will not advance your cause. You can always pivot pieces of the idea, but when you ask for actions or closed sales, they have to be concrete. In some meetings in the early days, I was so excited by a good meeting that I ended it with no concrete follow-up. I got out to the curb and said, "Damn, I have no idea what the next steps are!" If you go in with Jell-O ... you'll walk out with Jell-O ... and eating Jell-O is not a sustainable diet.

- **Be ready for disappointment and be open minded and prepared to ask why they are not interested.** Ask if you can change or adapt anything that would get them to buy (without begging). Go into these meetings with an understanding you can/might/will get rejected. The key is this: What are your pivots if that happens? Treat potential short meetings ("It's a no") and disappointments as a chance to learn at least one thing about your idea or service, about your competition, or about the person or company you are selling to.

- **Lastly, this truly is important in all sales call: referrals.** Again, whether these sales meeting go well or poorly, always ask: "Is there anyone at your company or another company that you think would be interested in this?" Sometimes you are just with the wrong person. Sometimes the person you are with does not need the service, but they have colleagues that might. When you get a referral, there are generally two ways to handle it.

1. In the first way of handling a referral, you can ask them if they will actually refer you with an email to the person you are being referred to, and ask that you are copied on the email. In this way, you know the referral was actually done and that you can also lead the next steps and follow up.

2. In the second way, you can be bolder and ask if you can send an email (which they approve) to the person you are being referred to and copy them. In this way you are leading the actions.

In either the first or second example above, you are taking action to get and move the referral forward. If you do not do either of these two, you run the risk of the referral never actually happening or even being real in the first place. Getting an action-oriented referral is as close as you can get to making a sale, so don't be afraid to go for it.

THE CLOSING STAGE

You can only eat what you kill! That sounds so brutal, doesn't it?

The reason this stage is different than the Lunching and Selling Stages is that you have to push people for an answer—a yes or a no. While it is sometimes fun to have a healthy prospect list that you have neither a yes or no from ("Hey, look at all the people and companies I have had lunch and initial sales calls with!"), it does not pay the bills. To use a metaphor, when you go to the butcher shop, they want to know if you want a hamburger, a steak, or Wagyu beef? Showing them your prospect list won't get you bupkis … just a blank stare from the butcher.

Here are some things to consider in this stage:

Shooting at ghosts: If someone has not called you back in a reasonable amount of time (a few weeks or so), then that is a *no* answer, not a no-answer-yet! In this stage, as hard as it is to imagine, it is actually better to hear *no* from a prospect than to keep hopefully believing they might join you later. It's better to have a tight prospect list of clients to close than a loose list of sales targets who are meandering about. You will see in the Lessons Learned section that I allowed this to fool me for too long.

When to take the shot: If you are going in for the kill, make sure you're OK'd to shoot! Be aware of budget and buying windows/cycles for clients. You need to be selling when people can buy. (For example, you would not go selling snow shovels door-to-door in the summer, right?) Same here. Understand when/how your prospects buy, and consider that timing.

Let me expand on something I learned when I was selling services to larger companies and that I briefly described above. Many companies typically have annual budget cycles and certain levels of signing authority. These are two different things.

First, recognize budget cycles and when money is available. Knowing when a company does their budgeting is important, as there are times you will want to get into their budget for the following time period. While they might not start the work now, they can get you into the budget with an estimated start date. Sometimes a client has interbudgetary money they can spend whenever they want, sort of a slush fund. Knowing and asking when they can budget and spend money is important. You may think you are trying to close business that would start in a month, for example, when the client is actually looking to put you in the budget for the next quarter or year. Know the differences and cycles.

Second, understand the prospect's signing authority and the signing/authorization process. Can they sign for a $50,000 service as their maximum, or does it need to go two levels higher to be accepted? There have been times I have met with a prospect and thought I had closed the sale, only to realize there were two more meetings required *and* a formal submission process.

> You will have to push people for a decision or action more than you might be comfortable with.

In the closing stage, you will have to push people for a decision or action more than you might be comfortable with. But that's why this stage is hard and high stakes. It is only when you have a signed contract or statement of work, cash/check, or another tangible commitment that you have really closed business.

A world-class founder and entrepreneur I have gotten to know very well is Wil Reynolds from SEER Interactive. Wil has grown a very successful marketing agency with large offices in Philadelphia and San Diego and has become a well-known speaker in areas he has become an expert in. As I was writing this book, Wil recounted the following story for me, which speaks to being accountable for closing business:

> When I was still starting out and had a handful of employees, I wasn't having the success rate I wanted when trying to close business. I worried that I was letting myself off the hook by thinking things like, "Maybe it's because I was too young," or "At times, the economy was bad," or other things that were out of my control. I remember one day, I decided that every month when I didn't hit my sales goals I would stand in the mirror and say, "Today, somewhere in the world, someone who does exactly what you do, sold the same service to a paying customer … but they just didn't buy it from you!" That reminded me from day one to take accountability for closing sales. Once I exhaled after saying that to myself, it became my reminder that tomorrow someone was going to buy what I am selling, and that I was going to work to improve. A bad economy or being too young (back then) was not something I could change, but making one more call, asking for referrals, or doubling down on a new strategy all are things I can control."

When you do get a no, don't think of it as a dead end, but rather as a cul-de-sac: you surely exit the street and can't drive on it for a while, but you have learned more about the street and will be better next time you visit. Just about every no is a lesson, and just about every no has the prospect of being a yes, with time and advancement of the business. Many of my first nos became yeses—over the years (not days).

LESSONS LEARNED

Referrals: Six Degrees of Separation

I have had more than a few situations where a sale was not going to happen, but a referral was asked for and provided. Once I got a chance to meet with the referral (it can take weeks or months), another sale did not happen, but another referral did. At this point, you get it ... out of the first five sales I got in one of my businesses, three out of the five were referral based, and two of those three referrals were twice-removed referrals. What I mean by "twice-removed" is that someone in company A referred me to someone in company B, and then company B referred me to yet another person in company C ... and finally, a sale was made! Referrals are gold, but it takes time to mine gold.

Closing a Sale Can Be Uncomfortable

During the Lunching Stage, which for me was roughly twenty meetings and a few months, I *thought* I was getting a lot of positive buying signals from prospects. As I stated, these were happy times because you are doing presales calls and learning about the offering and market needs, and not yet asking for a sale. All was good—or so I thought.

In particular, there were three prospects I had met with in the Lunching Stage that I was being ignored by in the Selling and Closing Stages. So I had to push! Some of that push was uncomfortable because it was with friends and former colleagues. I eventually settled on the action of sending them a challenging email that broached a now-or-never tone. It was uncomfortable to do that, and even though the email was friendly, it carried with it a let's-move-or-not tone to it.

I ended the email with a "signing off" from bothering them anymore tone, which was sort of a way of trying to turn the tables into them either pursuing me or telling me it was a no-sale. Either way, or as uncomfortable as it was, it was time to get a resolution. Ironically, and thankfully, all three of them emailed me back in thirty minutes and gave me real, tangible next steps.

The lesson learned: Don't be afraid to push a little. People know you are selling something and trying to survive. If you are professional and have earned the right to ask for the business, go for it. Remember, you can only eat what you kill.

A small list of solid prospects is better than a long list of maybes. In the early days, I overestimated the number of people who were kind during the Lunching Stage and then literally either did not meet with me again, took months to meet with me, or took months to tell me, "No" or "Not now." I had created what I thought to be a large active prospect list, when in fact all that I had was a list of meetings and mostly weaker prospects. I began to realize that it was hard for people to say no when I tried to close or advance business, especially face to face.

Chasing too many ghosts? I actually, counterintuitively, found it very liberating to learn who my exact prospects were and took solace out of that list being smaller than I liked, but being real. I learned it was better to have five tangible, real prospects than twenty prospects on a fictional list.

Key takeaway: Lunching, selling, and closing are stressful, tricky times. From what I have learned and heard other successful entrepreneurs talk about during this time in their journey, this is the time to be bold and ask for the business when you felt you had earned the right to ask.

Also, don't take a no-sale too much to heart; keep looking for the yeses, and don't be afraid to ask for referrals. If you have crafted the right product or service, there are customers out there ... you just need to find them and ask for the sale.

Law 6—Fail Fast and Fail Forward: Just Keep Moving

It's doubtful that anyone ever made a success of anything by waiting for all the conditions to be just right before starting.

Failing fast and failing forward are pretty simple. Understand there will be failures, and keep moving forward—no wasting time. Your laser focus on getting the idea/business/product right in Phase I was of primary importance. Nothing, personal or business, gets in the way of advancing it quickly in Phase II. Your passion for getting sales closed and the business moving is paramount for this law.

Failing forward is very visual for me. When you fail forward, you use it as a learning experience to advance things. You do it quickly, and you bounce back up to your feet almost before you hit the ground—nothing more and nothing less. Conversely, failing backward (on your ass) is where you spend too much time dusting off or wondering why that happened, or worse, feeling sorry for yourself or blaming others. No time for that …

> Failing forward, for me, is a very valid way to develop and progress an idea/business in the Idea and Launch Phases and, frankly, in life. In fact, I believe it is a requirement.

We have all been around glass-half-full people. They just see the best in things, the opportunities each situation presents, and they keep advancing. That is where you should try to be. Sadly, we have also been around the glass-half-empty people who tend to spend time blaming, bemoaning, and reliving the things that went wrong. Avoid those people, and try not to be

46

that person, as it will drain your soul.

Failing forward, for me, is a very valid way to develop and progress an idea/business in the Idea and Launch Phases and, frankly, in life. In fact, I believe it is a requirement. It's a requirement because you are going to have a lot of big and small failures in the beginning, and you have to just keep moving.

Let me clarify the "forward" piece of failing forward, though. Forward does not carry with it a warp speed that has you doing things that are done willy-nilly, randomly, in a poorly thought-out manner, or sloppily! Forward does not mean repeating the same mistakes. Forward actually carries with it the implication that you are *thinking things through and being deliberate in your actions.* The "fail" piece is just a fact that you are going to fail more often than not. Nowadays, you often hear the phrase "Go fast and break things." While "fail forward" has some of that in its DNA, fail forward is probably a few miles per hour slower, but advancing nonetheless.

You have to really listen every day to feedback you are getting in this phase also. In gathering the feedback, you then need to quickly think about how you want to adjust the idea or model by the next day. Some changes are small, while others are profound. Failing fast and forward is something you are doing in the quiet of your office or garage and not something you are exposing everyone to. This is where you are hunkered in, dusting off the failures, and then coming out to the world with the next version.

The "forward" is the next version of your product/service or approach after you failed. This is about actual changes you make to either your product/service or approach ... or both. Big changes are not a different version of a PowerPoint deck with a different spin. Big changes or adjustments to your approach are more profound and involve new materials, different components, improved options for pricing and usage, et cetera. You will know when you are making real (big) changes when you go back to people in the Lunching/Selling Stages and they say, "Wow, this has advanced a lot since we last met."

LESSONS LEARNED

Early on in one of my businesses, I was going after Procter & Gamble's pharmaceutical division. We really needed them to join in the benchmarking we were just beginning to do. I was able to get the name of the right buyer at P&G (or at least recommender), and I set out a plan to go after him. I sent a number of emails and letters/packets in street mail designed to attract him to speak with me on the phone. I was moving fast, and it was in the early days of trying to get a lot of sales calls in every day. I did not even think of flying out to Cincinnati from my Philadelphia base (first mistake).

I finally got his interest and had a conference call with him to review the benchmarking idea. After presenting the idea and service for my business *over the phone*, I thought the meeting went well. Not being in the room with a prospective client is never ideal because you cannot read body language, interest, and objections and get a feel for the meeting. But, heck, I was just starting out and moving fast (failing forward) and not wanting to spend the money to fly to Cincinnati. It's also worth noting there were no other pharmaceutical companies within 250 miles of Cincinnati, so I could not make a run out there and meet with a bunch of prospects. At that time, I also was enamored with my long prospect list and did not think I needed the effort to go full tilt after P&G (and, boy, was I wrong).

Two hours after the sales phone call, I got an email that read: "We are NOT going to move forward at this time—but thanks." *Ouch!* By operating under the fail-forward pirate flag, I had failed ... but was no "forward." Maybe this law was wrong!

Well, I let the dust and disappointment settle and

decided to follow up and ask why they decided to not move forward. P&G was nice enough to give me some feedback. The feedback made it clear to me that I did not describe the idea well enough to them and that I had blown it! They had said no for what I thought were the wrong reasons. How could I take this failure and move it forward?

I thought about options and decided I needed to see them face to face. I told them that I was going to be in the area, which was a total white lie, as described above, and asked if they would let me stop in when I was there.

They said yes to meeting with me again, so I booked my flight to be "in the area." I went back in, in person, and met with the same two people I had the phone call with weeks before. For that meeting I had adapted Law 4, the idea, more and was also able to directly address some of the objections they had. I also left time to listen to their thoughts and needs and read the room for good and bad signals. I thought the second sales meeting went well, and they said they would give it another look. Promising!

A few hours later, upon returning on the one-hour flight from Cincinnati to Philadelphia, as I walked through the airport, I listened to a voice mail from P&G giving me the yes and the go-ahead! In failure, we had found a way to move forward and had done it pretty quickly. To this day, I can tell you exactly where I was standing in the vast Philadelphia airport and the elation I had at learning to fail fast and fail forward. In retrospect, it is probably the most significant win I have ever had as an entrepreneur.

Epilogue: The P&G sale gave us the third client to join us. We were getting close to the five clients we needed to get the business going. Also, and probably more relevant, was that this was the first client none of us had ever known, as our first two clients were former colleagues who threw us a bone and joined us. But P&G—P&G was a business stranger, and they had bought our idea/service after initially saying no. We had turned them around. That was *the moment* we knew we had something with this business and idea!

Key takeaway: Fail forward! Move quick, understand things will break, be deliberate and thoughtful, but keep moving and adapting. You'll get a few failures as you move forward, but you will also get more winners.

PHASE III—THE GROWTH PHASE: HOW TO GET IT MOVING

If the Launch Phase, which we just outlined, was about getting the rocket off the ground and into orbit, the Growth Phase is about taking a few laps around the planet and proving you can fly.

There are thousands of books on the art and science of selling, and even more about growing a business. There are college degrees and master's programs on sales, and countless seminars and courses centered growing a business. What follows is much briefer and is based on things I learned, mostly the hard way, and had to learn quickly to grow my businesses. They are also based on the experiences and stories from fellow entrepreneurs. You might call these the hard-knocks lessons for growing a new idea/venture/product and an abbreviated but focused version of those books, courses, and degrees.

The Growth Phase comes at about months 6 through 9, based upon my experiences and the experience of other entrepreneurs, and can typically last through months 15 to 24. Generally speaking, you're past the first six months of the Idea and Launch Phases, in which you have proven you have something, but by no means are you out of the woods. Some of your nervousness about this being the right idea/approach has subsided, but you're still nervous about the mid- and long-term success and size of the venture. This phase is not necessarily about scaling the business, although you will have to build some processes and systems to grow, as scaling the business will come after the first two years or so. This is really about going faster with what you have and getting what you absolutely need.

I stress "what you need" versus "what you want." You may need help. So you go out and either hire people in as economical a manner as possible (revenue sharing, low fees with bonuses, and so forth) or bring on consulting/part-time help. You may *want* to hire people instead, but frankly, you do not need the initial headache that full-time hiring brings along with it (health benefits, offices, expenses). In the Growth Phase, you are staying lean and mean but doing what you have to do to grow!

It is often said that "revenue is the best cologne/perfume." It is. When you are growing, you have the resources and confidence to add anything you need and some of the things you want. If you are not growing and lack cologne, well then, you start to take on a smell.

Law 7—Decision Makers: Finding the Corner Offices

The quickest path to business success lies
with getting to people who need you.

If you are not talking to someone who can decide to buy your services so you can grow your business, you should either be working your way toward that person, or you might be wasting time. Always diagnose as fast as you can whether you have the decision maker in front of you. There are a few ways to do that:

- Ask how decisions, like the one about buying your product or service, are made. Being curious about this will help you understand where and who you are with during the selling cycle.

- Cite other companies in stating what their process for this was or is. That will have your prospective buyer outline how their company's process compares.

- Be bold enough to ask, at the right time in a meeting, who would be the person to make the final decision on this.

- Perform "office triage." On your walk through the office for your meetings, you should be able to triage some degree of hierarchy. That might help you with understanding if you are with decision makers.

Let's face it: getting to a decision maker is *much* easier said than done. Sometimes it is dependent on the great (or not-so-great) network you have. You may have a career, network, association, or alma mater that provides fertile ground for you to get to decision makers. Or you may be starting with the proverbial phone book and email addresses (nowadays, that's LinkedIn) of your targets and will need multiple meetings to get to the decision makers. Either way, you need to get started, so here are some thoughts.

REFERRALS

As I outlined previously, referrals are simply the best way to get meetings. Sometimes it is an internal referral, where you know someone at a lower level than the decision makers, and they will sponsor/refer you up the line. At other times, it is an external referral, where someone in either another department or another company knows the person and they can refer you to him or her. Whatever the mechanics are, always try to look for referrals.

The referral trail occasionally goes cold. You will find people who will be generous in trying to help you out with referrals and others who will provide little assistance. I can attest to a number of people who I felt owed me favors, and I was counting on them for help/referrals but got nowhere. While those referral trails and expectations went cold and were hurtful and disappointing, it made me understand a few simple things that I will share. I share these not to be negative but to maybe help you identify if and when help is truly on the way or it is not.

First, there are a number of people in your sphere of colleagues and contacts who—no matter how much you have done for them in the past and present—are just takers. They do not seem to have the self-awareness that life is a two-way street, and they only see one-way signs leading to themselves. Don't let the disappointment you may find with them make you crazy; it is what it is. You might, as I did and do, not be too responsive in the future when they ask for help, but don't get too crazy or bummed out by it.

Second, some people are sort of cowards. There are people who will always be afraid to stick their neck out for you or anybody. Anything that would jeopardize or wobble their security is a non-starter. They look at providing a referral as an unnecessary risk. Once again, let it go, or instead of asking for a referral, ask for some coaching on how to get to some other people or what would resonate with the decision makers.

Third, there are people who will sit on the sidelines for a while to first make sure you are going to be a success before providing a referral or help. While that does not do you a lot of good right now, when you need it, it is what it is, and they can become fans down the road. Play with the long game in mind.

And fourth and lastly, while this may make you cringe, there are people out there who might want to see you fail. It's terrible to say, but it is human nature for some people to not want to see others achieve success greater than theirs. They will verbally encourage you and even feign help, but they will quietly stand aside, hoping things don't work out. You will typically only find out about these folks later when they murmur something like, "I thought you were not going to make it" or "I wanted to wait to make sure you were going to make it before … " Once again, let it be.

> Play with the long game in mind.

While the four examples above may worry you at first to think referrals are impossible to get, they are not. I guess my summary would be that for every referral you get, there are two to three non-referrals you might experience, and that is OK. You will see, as the years pass, that you can make allowances for folks you thought would help and never did. It's all good!

Making Your Way to Decision Makers:
The Stepping-Stone Meeting

On the way to decision makers, sometimes you will (you should) set up meetings, knowing the purpose of the meeting is just to get a referral or test your idea versus actually selling something in that meeting. Knowing this in advance and preparing for a stepping-stone meeting is different than a true sales meeting. In a stepping-stone meeting, you are trying to see if the product/service is a fit, ask questions about other services or competitors, and tailor your offering for the next meeting. You are also trying to understand the approval and budgeting process I spoke about in Phase II.

While I wrote briefly about how to take action on referrals, allow me to expand here a little more. The best way to get a referral, in my opinion, is by having the referring person email the person you are being referred to with you copied in. I prefer email because it is documented, tangible, and actionable. Even better, if the email can copy you, then you have hit referral gold. In this gold scenario, you 1) know the referral happened, 2) understand the context, 3) have the email of person you are being referred to, and 4) can take the lead on the actions. So, when asking for a referral, be specific about the help you need, and suggest the best way to do it.

If you want to go one step further in the example above, you can offer to write a draft of the referral email for the person doing the referring to make it *easy* for them. You will also cut down the amount of time you are waiting for a referral by doing it quickly. I know this may seem overly detailed, but I have learned hard lessons by not being detail oriented with these situations. It would be like a gold miner allowing gold so spill through their system and not truly capturing everything they were after. This is where details matter.

Of course, you need to be chill and not be a stalker with the referral, and be somewhat patient—but not too patient. Remember, the person you are being referred to has no idea you were "coming" and was not sitting in their office waiting for you. So make sure you give it the right amount of time to make it work.

Here is a warning about someone taking your materials to the decision maker without you. Be very careful about a person wanting to take your product/service to their boss without you being there. There were and are plenty of times when someone says, "Can you send me the materials, and I will take it to my boss?" In my experience, when I have let someone introduce our product or service to their boss without me being present, nine out of ten times, they come back with "I showed my boss, and they were not interested." Argh! What are you supposed to do with that? Dead end! What I try to do in these cases is offer that I will be more than happy to put the presentation together, let them tweak it, and *join* them in a meeting with the boss. If they want to send something along to the boss in an email to lay the groundwork, I offer to write the email draft for them and ask that I am copied. Simply put, I try to practice the rule that nobody takes our "sales stuff" and sells it for me without me being there. Either just refer me, or take me along—I'll do the explaining! This does not always work, but be forewarned about allowing it to happen a lot and expecting good results.

When Referrals Are Not Happening, You Have to Take Other Actions

Cold calls. A cold call is the simple act of dialing a person's phone number (office or cell) and trying to talk about your product or service when/if they answer the call. We all get them, and I would portend we all dislike them and consider them a pretty low form of making contact. That said, for those companies that do them, it is a numbers game, in which they hope that one in a hundred results in something. I do understand that this can be an effective manner to get prospects and would grant those companies the understanding that it is an effective form of marketing. I would also understand the need to try and cold-call a handful of prospects if you are getting nowhere with them. So, while I am about to throw cold water on cold-calling (pun intended), there is a time and place for it, and I understand that.

That said, personally and professionally, I never, ever, ever do them. In the professional services businesses or sales roles I have been in during my career and entrepreneurial journey, I have found there was little place for them.

First, frankly, I am an absolute lightweight when it comes to doing that type of thing. I am an admitted coward. I am just not brave enough to pick up the phone and cold-call someone I do not know, or barely know. If I had to do this, my stomach would be in knots, and I would suck at it. I remember going for a job interview a few years out of college, thinking I wanted to be a personal financial planner. Good field with a chance to help people manage their money and putting my financial and analytical skills to good use, right? Well, I went on the interview to the financial planning company, and initially I was psyched. They had beautiful office space, all the best leather furniture, mahogany walls, and baroque music playing in the background. It felt right! Then during my interview, they said to me that I had to make a list of one hundred friends and relatives and start calling them once I started working there. What? I had to either cold-call or just plain call all the people I knew best and speak to them live? Needless to say, I never went back there.

A second thing about cold calls: I think they are lame. They fail to represent the tone and branding that any company I have been associated with would employ. Needing to have your employees or any of the cold-calling, lead-generation services make cold calls just feels desperate and undifferentiated to me.

Lastly, I believe 100 percent of people really dislike getting cold calls. It brings out the worst in me when I get them, and I hang up. I deplore them when they somehow come masked enough so that you answer the phone, only to realize you have been duped and it is a cold call.

Yet here is a life preserver on cold calls in case you have to do them. You had better develop either a world-class method for doing it or have such an amazing service/product that people are dying to listen. I do not come from the cold-calling world, so my points on this matter are exhausted.

Emails. If I am an admitted coward regarding making cold calls, I am Braveheart in sending emails to sales prospects (chuckle). While I will admit to being creative in my justification for sending emails, I have just found better success at using the right emails with the right information. Here are some tips that I use.

Make good use of the subject line in the email, probably referring to something or someone that will resonate. Use the subject line in a practical way (not hyperbole), and describe either what you have or the benefit of it! Some examples from one my businesses:

- "How do other pharmaceutical companies do 'it'?" This was my advisory company's fundamental idea and positioning, and we chose to ride and use it a lot! This subject line was meant to strike a chord and curiosity with the recipient, hoping to generate some momentum to get the next step: a meeting.

- "Benchmarking information about your peers ... and

insights" (a similar tone, and not overstated). The hope here was that it would also pique curiosity and speak to a person's natural desire to understand the market space.

- "Information for your planning season." Every position has a planning season when they can use additional information to help them formulate and support their plans within their company or business. This subject line was meant to serve them, and in that, to try to create interest.

- "Jim recommended we should meet because ... " Nothing fancy here. Stick with the referring person's name and why it happened.

Here, in my opinion, are some bad uses of the subject line. Take it from me; I have tried and failed using the following techniques:

- "We can help your company succeed!" Really ... really? Making bold statements like that will do nothing but get you deleted—and possibly blocked.

- "I promise to take only fifteen minutes of your time." You're already starting off weak and begging. If you got the referral, there is no need to beg or set unwelcome parameters. If you have something, you will need thirty to sixty minutes to describe it.

- "Act now ... limited-time offer!" In a B2B world, this is silly and makes you look cheap ... and possibly desperate.

Here's my last word about emails and the length/body of them. All emails should fit on the screen, and in fact have room on the screen so it does not look like a five-page note. State your email case simply, and leave the explaining for the meeting. It should look crisp and eye-catching. The beauty of email is you can also try a few different formats on different people and see what works and what does not. Said another way, don't use the same email on your entire next sales wave. Try a few different approaches to see what works best, and then go with that approach.

"Street mail"—hard copy. Now, here is one I like. I have personally become a big fan of handwritten notes, street mail, and overnight mail/packages. In today's digital world, there is a lot of digital clutter, but not a lot of business-to-business street mail. Call me a Luddite, but here goes.

I get more than 150 emails a day and countless other forms of digital communication from friends and family and people trying to get my attention. I'm digitally underwater. That said, when I get street mail with any type of handwritten letter, especially in the office, I look at it and give it consideration. In the early days of one of my businesses (see *The Diary of Year One* on my website at www.stephenegerard.com), I would send ten to twenty street mail letters a week to targets in the attempt of getting a look. I simply believed that street mail gave me a decent shot at someone paying at least a little attention to my message.

Street mail (hard copy) has a chance of surviving and making it to the target, whereas I think email does not nowadays with spam and junk filters. We all get some satisfaction out of hitting the delete button in email before reading a single word of an email. But with business street mail, I feel someone at least has to open it, look at it, and process it, especially if it is professional, interesting, and well done. Remember, I am talking about business-to-business mail, not the mail, brochures, catalogs, and offers that flood your home mailbox. I believe fewer and fewer businesses are sending street mail to other businesses as forms of solicitation.

Quick snail-mail story: At the end of my first full year in business,

I got a call from Allergan Pharmaceuticals in Irvine, California, from someone who literally said, "I have had your letter and brochure on my desk for months, and I finally said I need to contact you or throw it out." My street mail tactic had worked. It literally sat on his desk for months—talk about advertising! We spoke about what my company was offering and then set a meeting. I flew out to Allergan in California, and we ended up getting them as a client and kept them for fifteen-plus years! As an added benefit, I ended up being out in Orange County so much we bought a home in Laguna Beach. Cheers to the Luddite! I can also attest to other meetings we had in the early days in which we could see our letter or brochure on the credenza of a person's office or that they carried into our sales meeting.

Handwritten thank-you notes. When is the last time you got one of these?

After you meet with people, send handwritten thank-you notes. In my estimation, only one in over a hundred people/companies do this. So by doing it, you're bound to be different and, I would proffer, appreciated. Get some nice letterhead done, and do it religiously. In my first few years of business, this was money well spent and also represented a quality and distinction I wanted for my company. I got many comments about this over the years, all positive. Send street mail thank-you notes, not email.

As an added thought on thank-you notes, if someone else was also helpful in getting a meeting set up (e.g., the exec's administrative assistant) or helping with a referral, make sure to send them a handwritten thank-you also. It is the right thing to do *and* goes a long way to the next meeting and getting next steps in place quickly. When you're meeting with people, caring about them matters, and saying thanks is a good thing!

What to Do When You Are in the
Decision Maker's Office or Cubicle

Pay attention; look around. When I am in someone's office or cubicle, I naturally look for other connections and points of commonality with just about everyone I meet, business or pleasure. For me, it comes somewhat natural to be curious about people. While I am certainly in someone's office to talk business—and, let's face it, sell or advance something—I am genuinely interested in other things about the person.

While you have to be careful and earn the right to talk nonbusiness, especially with people you are just meeting for the first time, I like to look around the office and see what people are interested in outside of business. I find common ground with people in areas like children, travel, alma mater, sports, and prior work pathways that are typically on display in their offices. How did they get to where they are today? What do they do in their spare time? Do they have kids, a family?

When I can strike up a conversation about that, once again at the right and appropriate time, I find it just makes doing business more pleasant. Knowing a little about the person also gives you other avenues for follow-up than just business. If you can follow up about vacation spots, sports, alma mater, and other nonbusiness things, you tend to set yourself out from the crowd. Frankly, it makes doing business a little more enjoyable. Don't get me wrong; I am not going to go

> Making a sale, for a meaningful product or service (i.e., an expensive one with a long implementation) takes three to five meetings with a person and other stakeholders in a company.

overboard and try to make it feel like I have been lifelong friends with a person I am just meeting for the first few times—that's creepy. I am also not going to overly dwell on it and keep hammering it. I am simply going to use it as another point of connection in easing the way for them to be comfortable with me.

Create follow-ups. Even if you know the answer to every question someone raises in a meeting, I would advise you to leave one or two for follow-ups. While you naturally want to handle every question or issue on the spot, I would proffer that you don't handle everything on the spot. I have learned through detailed metrics and years of experience that making a sale, for a meaningful product or service (i.e., an expensive one with a long implementation) takes three to five meetings with a person and other stakeholders in a company. Knowing that going in, you realize that creating a good follow-up that a prospect wants to hear about creates another touch. Touches (meetings) and multiple contacts in the sales process are good. In the early days, in meetings in which I answered all the questions in a first meeting, I was left with "So now what?" While it might be easy to dream of one-call closes, I did not find that to be the case—hence the desire to create follow-ups and multiple meetings. It may have slowed things down a bit, but it got me a high percentage of closes once we got deep into the sales process. I have often feigned that I would follow up in three days with answers, even when I knew the answers on the spot.

Now, don't get me wrong. If you are in a closing meeting (in my businesses, this might typically be the third, fourth, or fifth meeting), then you may not want to create a follow-up. You may want to provide the answers and then ask for the business. If, though, this is your first or second meeting, think about creating a good reason for a meaningful follow-up.

LESSONS LEARNED

The Referral Story

It was our second year in business, and we were doing a small benchmark for Novartis Pharmaceuticals, one of the top five pharmaceutical companies in the world. As we were winding down our first benchmark project, the decision maker of the group had a proposition for us. He said, "If this goes well and you deliver on this work, I want to start a benchmark in another department I lead." He went on to say, "And if we can get that going, I will help you start it and get you referrals to colleagues in other companies." Wow!

Here was a client not only offering to help us start an entirely new service line (benchmark) in another department where we had never done work before, but he was also willing to help us get referrals from other companies. As you might imagine, we did a terrific job for him, and upon completion, we went to see him. In our meeting he extolled the wonderful work we did and then proceeded to put together a working group of his staff to help us shape the new service offering and also start to reach out to colleagues they knew in other companies. They became our sales force in a way!

We handheld the referral process by writing all the referral emails for the Novartis team, and we made sure they were crafted in a manner that would result in an in-person meeting. Within a month or two of working with them, we had a working prototype of the new offering and referrals and meetings with many of the top ten pharma companies in the world. That sort of thing does not happen every day, but it can happen when you do good work for decision makers. They not only make a difference in their company, but they also can make a difference in your company and in an entire industry.

As a side note, this customer and his team became lifelong clients, and when they went on to other pharmaceutical companies in the industry, they called us and brought us along and into their new companies.

Key takeaway: Referrals, the right sales approaches, and great clients, done the right way, *are magic.*

Law 8—The Phone Never Rings: Take Action

Success in sales is finding a cure for the cold shoulder.

—Robert Orbey

I covered a lot of ground in the prior law (Law 7) about tactics and thoughts on selling, but I think a few other things are worth mentioning. The main theme of this law is obvious. Nobody is going to call you and make things happen for you. You may have folks imply that help is on the way, but it rarely is. I learned this lesson the hard way in the early days, when I really thought people were going to call me back. The phone will ring, but it will be with people either cold-calling you or trying to sell you something.

BEWARE THE COFFEE SHOP ENTREPRENEURS

Maybe it's me or just the way I go about ideating things and getting things done, but I need a place that gives me peace and quiet and a place to focus with minimal distractions. If I cannot find that space in my home or office, or I need a change of scenery, you will find me at the local library or closest university library. I go there and try to find the farthest corner of the library and sit at a desk where I will not be disturbed or tempted to be distracted. Whether I was studying for the CPA exam or my MBA early on in my career, or trying to get work done, libraries (quiet places) are my happy places for producing good work and thinking. With that as my basis, I naturally have a bias toward people who seem to be in places, like coffee shops, where the exact opposite happens. In a coffee shop, there are tons of distractions and a myriad of ways to not get a lot done. While we all have

69

the need for some action and camaraderie, there is a time and place for that.

So my warning to midcareer entrepreneurs: If you need to get a lot or work done, stay out of the coffee shop. Nobody in the coffee shop cares about your venture, and I might insinuate their only interest in your efforts might be to get a job. The last thing you are doing when you start a business is handing out jobs. Allow me to be a little crass as a way of warning you about not being that person, and also not thinking that person can be of great help to your efforts. The coffee shop entrepreneur typically posts up in Starbucks or the local coffee place, looking important and busy and often talking too loudly on the phone (about "deals"), when they should be at home or in another setting trying to find clients or honing ideas. All of those things take peace and quiet; the action will come later.

STRATEGIC PARTNERSHIPS: FORGET 'EM EARLY ON!

With the exception of maybe a few business in which some type of partnership might make sense, all of the entrepreneurial ventures I have been around required the founder(s) to lift the business off the ground themselves. Once you have shown you have a real, hopefully thriving business is when partnerships might be worth spending time on. But when it is still early, focus on what you, and you alone, can control.

> When it is still early, focus on what you, and you alone, can control.

In the early days, you may find other companies/people who believe there is an opportunity to partner. That partnership can come in the form of joint product offerings in which you combine aspects of a few products or services, or in other shapes and sizes. Almost all the time, I found these to be a waste of time, especially in the early days where you are trying to survive and grow your business. I found these "initiatives" to be a thinly vailed tactic used by another company wanting to partner with me on *my* clients. Said another way, these reach-outs feigned some degree of strategic alignment and a higher good, while what they really wanted was access to my clients. I rarely found they wanted to share their clients with me. Even worse, under the guise of partnership, they were looking to do consulting work for me or get a job with me. Don't get me wrong; I have no problem hiring good consultants and employees, but coming to me under the guise of a "partnership" with little to offer is off-putting. In summary, I rarely (maybe never) found the time spent on strategic partnerships to be fruitful.

In summary, save the big ideas and outside partnerships for another day. In the early days, run solo in the sense of you being in complete control of your idea and your business. Once you have success and a great client base, you can pick your head up and see if partnerships offer anything.

SOME ADDITIONAL SALES AND MARKETING TACTICS

Here are some other creative ways I have used to take action and reach out to people that I really wanted to get meet with:

I'm in the area! I'd always offer the "I'm in the area" line to get a commitment for someone to meet with me because I felt it made the commitment a little lighter. I would do this even if it took me a cross-country plane flight to get in "the area." I'd make every effort to offer a light approach to meeting with me versus saying, "I will fly out to meet with you." I was looking for this response: "Sure! You are in the area; stop in."

Street mail. Retreading ground here, but a well-timed letter, package, or something in street mail has a good chance of getting a positive response, versus email or phone messages. At the risk of overdoing it, there were a number of times I would use FedEx, UPS, or USPS overnight packages to really get attention and rise above normal mail.

FOMO: Fear of missing out. It's human nature to not want to miss out on something good or new. When I felt I had something unique, new, or interesting to offer, I would highlight that in my reach out to people. Sometimes, it was as simple as making sure a person knew I was meeting with a number of their peers: "Hey, I met with Marty and Sharon, former colleagues of yours, and we had a good chat about *X*. Thought you would be interested." FOMO got me a lot of meetings because nobody likes to miss out or be lagging.

YAMO: You are missing out. If it's human nature to fear missing out, then it's DEFCON 5 to not want to miss out on something that is happening. Once I got things up and running with clients, I would make sure some of my prospects knew it was happening. Sometimes, it was as simple as making sure a person knew I was doing work with a number of their peers or competitors: "Hey, I met with Jim and Margaret, and they are moving forward with the *X*. We are a go!" FOMO got me a lot of meetings, but YAMO got me a lot of clients.

"Good for your career"—making the meeting appeal personal. When I genuinely felt I had something good and something worth sharing, I would occasionally take the approach of "Hey, this is something you need to know about in your role with your company." It is human nature to want to manage one's career, especially with information. While I would never overpromise what I was doing and what it could do for people, I did feel it was something valuable.

Since it had value, I felt I could make the "good-for-you" assertion and deliver on it. I found that people will take action to be in the know and be smarter/better at what they do in their careers. Nobody loses when you can deliver on that.

Level up ("I know the boss above you"). If I knew I could get to the person above the person to whom I was reaching out, I let them know it. I would always do it in a genuine, nonthreatening way, but I would do it: "Hey, I know Jimmy [your boss] and told him I would reach out, but I wanted to meet with you first." I always found giving someone this courtesy was appreciated, and while it may have slowed me down a little, it made closing a sale easier. It was a case of going slower to invariably go faster.

The trick to this is that you need to let the lower-level person understand they are not getting control of the meeting with the boss. The meeting with them is a pure courtesy and never takes on the tone of needing their approval or sponsorship. It's a fine line to walk but can be handled in the way you say things: "When I meet with James, your boss" versus "If you like this, we can take it to James."

During those meetings with the underling, you can judge whether you want to invite that person into the boss meeting and whether they can be a supporter or not. I have seen it work well and badly when they are in the meetings, and also work well and badly when they are not invited to the meetings. This is a trust-your-gut call—tricky stuff.

Conference stalker. There were times I would go to an industry conference with the express (only) purpose of seeing a few prospects in the meetings or halls. I would work to create a casual "bump-into" and then try for the proverbial side meeting or beer later in the day. I guess you could also call this technique redundant to the "I am in the area" tactic mentioned above (literally)!

Fridays are for closing. While it may sound obvious now, we found that the best day to make contact with people, whether a reach out for a meeting, a next step in a decision, or closing a sale was on Fridays! It's obvious, but everybody is in a good mood on Fridays. They have hopefully had a productive week and are ready for happy hour or getting home to the family and friends. Even more specific, we found that between 10:00 a.m. and 2:00 p.m. was the ideal window of time. The rationale there was the day had already started, but they were not on cruise control for the weekend yet. It also gave them a few hours to get back to us. Nowadays, with many companies having summer hours when people might be gone from the office by 2:00 p.m. on a Friday, you may have to adjust and experiment with the best time window for those companies. The same holds true for companies that have work-from-home policies. Understand the rhythm of your target clients, and apply the "when-they-are-happy" rule!

Fridays are for closing.

If Fridays were the best for successful reach-outs, as you might imagine, Mondays and Tuesdays were not. In the beginning of the week, people are hunkered down getting to their to-do lists. Trying to get attention or traction or close deals at the beginning of the week can be a nonstarter.

LESSONS LEARNED

FedEx-ing and Email (Double-Barreled Outreach)

In the early days, I would send five to ten FedEx packages a week, typically on a Tuesday or Wednesday, so they landed on the desk of my prospect on Thursday or Friday. I would then shoot them an email on Friday addressing what I sent. I was working from the premise that a) street mail and overnight envelopes get noticed and read in combination, with b) Fridays are for closing or getting attention.

I firmly believe that this double-barreled approach had to get the attention of my prospect. If I got no response, I would wait a month or so and do it again (with new materials). My repetition for this tactic was probably three times, max. After that, I would have to try other mechanisms. When I combined this with referrals, FOMO and YAMO, and "I'm in the area," I felt as though there was almost no target I could not get to. It was not all easy, though, but changing things up and being persistent works out if you balance persistence with patience (more on that in Law 15).

The Level-Up Approach Can Backfire

There was at least one time where the "level up" ("Hey, I know your boss, but I'll meet with you first") backfired on me. I share this to emphasize that not all tactics and approaches work.

Some background: I knew the president of a midsize ($500 million in revenue) pharmaceutical company and knew I could easily get to him for a meeting. I also had a fair degree of confidence that it would go well and he would be an early buyer. That said, I wanted to provide the courtesy of having a lower-level person meet with me first, versus going right to the top. I was trying to play nice and work my way up the chain, even though these were the early days of the business and I needed to move quickly.

The backfire reaction: I reached out to the person (the lower-level position than the president), letting them know I knew the GM very well but wanted to give them the courtesy of meeting first. I had never met this person and by all accounts felt they were a B- or maybe C-league player. They dodged me for months, canceling meetings, often last minute and once when I was actually in the lobby for a scheduled meeting. They kept making excuses not to meet with me. These delays amounted to months of missed meetings. They were really giving me the runaround—and I was doing this by my choice as a courtesy!

I stayed patient and finally met with them. In that meeting, they barely gave me a chance to talk about the offering before shitting all over it. They really had no interest in any outside thinking and wanted to be left alone to do their job with no intrusions. It was sort of "the fewer questions asked about what they were doing, the better." I think it was also an issue of not wanting me or my offering being in the building because I knew the president.

Subsequent to that meeting, they did everything they could to sabotage the sale process with the president. It finally got so contentious that I had to convince the president that I was not getting a fair shake and that I would take on the work for a money-back-guarantee approach. If they felt that what I provided was not of value, it would be free. If it was of value, then I would be paid the agreed-upon amount. I had to back the lower-level person into a corner and neutralize all of their excuses for not working with me.

We finally got the job, and he continued to stall, undermine, and sabotage all that we did. We stayed cool and worked through it. It took two to three times longer than it should have, but we got the work done. We ended up producing a really great analysis for them and provided a solid set of recommendations to multiple executives and the president at the company. The work was well received. In the end, we got paid the full amount and were able to manage to keep him out of our way in the future. That said, he never became a fan.

Key takeaway: The moral of the story is that this tactic cost me time, but it was still the better way to go, rather than going right to the president. Sometimes sacrificing speed can deliver a better outcome ... it's just frustrating. Also, I am not advocating that a single tactic will always work; think of the tactics outlined here as a variety of ammunition that can be used singularly or altogether if needed. Pick and choose, and be consistent, and you will succeed.

Law 9—Being Accountable versus Hopeful or Lucky

Hope is not a strategy. Luck is not a factor. Fear is not an option.

—James Cameron

If you use the word "hope" in a sentence when it comes to selling or advancing your business, you'd better be really lucky or have a trust fund. Now, I am being a bit glib with the word *hope* here. What I am trying to convey here is that the entirety of succeeding or failing is on your back and that hope won't get you there. The *hope* word, for me, is a passive way of thinking (hoping) things will advance. It's sort of a "things will fall into place" mentality, which at its extreme could create a sort of laziness.

When you are launching a business it will require deliberate actions and full accountability, versus hope or luck. While I am sure you know that, I have also seen some early entrepreneurs start to see some positive things happen and then sit back, "hoping" they will fall into place. For them, hope—and what I perceived as the accompanying laziness or the complacency hope might afford—caused them to fail. Hope replaced accountability.

> Hope—and what I perceived as the accompanying laziness or the complacency hope might afford—caused them to fail. Hope replaced accountability.

Here are some things, if I were an investor in your company, I would hope (pun intended) I was *not* hearing:

- "I'm hoping that person gives me a good referral. They promised!"
- "I'm hoping the next version of the service is better."
- "I'm hoping this strategic partnership lands me some clients."
- "I'm hoping I see that person at a conference so I can get time with them."

Once again, I am being a little glib and trying to differentiate intent versus hope/luck. While we can all use a little luck, I generally find that luck and hope in the early days are earned and don't just happen upon us. They are earned through an unrelenting drive and sweat to make things happen. In later years, when your business has created some momentum and a flywheel effect, you may accrue some luck and garner some hope. But in the early days, hope and luck are generally strangers or infrequent visitors to the business.

Always run through the tape and the finish line, never taking victory for granted. If you are trying to close a sale, map out all the possible actions you can take, not just the first one, the easiest one, or the most hopeful one. Map out the what-ifs. If they do not respond (like you *hope*), then have options and actions at the ready.

This law and its ramifications are probably some of the biggest differences in being out on your own as an entrepreneur versus being in a larger, more established company (see the chapter at the end of the book on the difference between entrepreneurship and intrapreneurship). You can do a bit of hoping when you are in the latter in a large company, but you have no room for hoping in the former. The proverbial buck, and the need to make money so you can buy food for your family, rests with you and solely you.

When you are in your own venture, there is no "they"; there is just you! Don't let hope in the building and work tirelessly to cover every possibility and angle. When you do that, you will still lose a few, but you will also win and control more. Hope and luck are not welcome bedfellows.

I know I am beating this one into the ground, but it's only my way of expounding on not falling into a complacency trap or surrendering to the context. When you start to surrender to the context, you allow outside influences to play a factor in your success. You start setting up alleyways (excuses, escape hatches) for not succeeding. In this surrender, you hear things from people like the following:

- *To achieve the goal, I need to get every one of the targets closed.* The surrender here is that you need them all. You are probably not going to get them all, so you should have had three times the number of prospects ready and in the pipeline to achieve the goal.

- *If the manufacturer does not get me the prototypes, I won't have anything to show.* The surrender here is that you are relying on one person/company for your success. You should have had a backup manufacturer (no matter what it costs you) and another alternative to view/touch/feel the product.

- *If the person/company misses the deadline, I am screwed.* This is the same as the last one. You surrendered your success to an outside party on a tight timeline. You should have had a flexible timeline for an earlier delivery and/or a later sales meeting.

So the point of not using the word *hope* (or *luck*) is a metaphor for taking full control of your destiny and being 100 percent accountable. If or when you have control, there is no need for hope. Don't get me wrong; be hopeful—just don't rely on it.

LESSONS LEARNED

Hope Differs from Reality

Keeping a detailed account of sales targets and prospects was a religion for us in our business. From the early days and for years to come, we kept detailed sales-pipeline reports for the prospects and sales targets we had. We called it the gap report because it represented the gap between our current revenue and the planned/goal revenue. Frankly, I would hope that is pretty standard for any business, especially a professional or high-end services business with finite, high-value prospects.

The mistake I made in the early days was that I was proud of our long list of active prospects. It felt good to have a large sales funnel and to keep reviewing how many targets and meetings we might be having. The problem was that the list was based more on hope than reality and that I was kidding myself with quantity versus quality/reality. There was a lack of accountability to having a realistic sales pipeline.

We began to realize this when we found we were recycling the same names of targets for weeks and months on end. We were like a broken record of the same sales prospects with little progress. We were highly organized but a tad delusional—due to hope and lack of honest accountability!

We ended up developing a rule or two to keep ourselves more accountable:

Sixty days and done: If a sales target is on your list for roughly sixty days and is not advancing and progressing (or flaming out), take it off the list. It is a hope or a mirage, and neither of these belong on valid sales lists for long. In these cases we were doing more hoping than living with the reality of a thin/insufficient prospect list. When we became more accountable, we started seeing a real sales funnel and had a better gauge of the things we needed to focus on.

Naming names (who and when): If you can not name the specific people you are targeting, their roles, and an idea of their needs, then you can't keep them in the sales funnel too long. There is no "hoping" that this information will just magically fall in your lap. You have to have imminent plans to get the information, which you will then need to take action on.

Ruthlessly taking a carving knife to a sales prospect list so you have a clear view of reality was a lesson on accountability that took us some time to figure out.

Activity Differs from Results

One last example of the adage that "activities do not equal results" revolves around office space. When I say office space, I mean shopping for it, picking it, negotiating it, decorating it, and so forth. My point is that this activity is *very* time consuming, and there is a right time and a wrong time to do it.

Unfortunately, I have met a number of early entrepreneurs who have wasted an inordinate amount of time on this activity when they should have been selling, growing, innovating, scaling their business, and letting the nice/ great office space come later. As a real example and having watched others fail at this, I kept things lean and mean in the beginning, and I had the following "offices":

Years 1 and 2: No office. I used my house and the local university's library. I found that using a far-flung table in the morning in a local university library to be a really inexpensive way to meet with people. I never spent a dime or wasted a minute on offices. I also did a barter deal for a desk, copier, and some administrative support with a small group of former colleagues who had started a small ad agency in Princeton, New Jersey. I helped them with certain aspects of their business and bartered for an office address, a desk, use of the copier and conference room, and some support. I did not want to be using my home address for the business address and felt that a Princeton office address would convey the brand I wanted to develop. It also gave me a place to get out of the house and feel more businesslike. (To provide context, my annual revenue was $175,000 in year 1 and then $775,000 in year 2.)

Year 3: I rented a small two-bedroom apartment in a local town near me. I spent a half day looking around and leased it on the spot when I found it. The space was not even zoned for offices and was a two-bedroom apartment with a small kitchen, a small dining room (which became a conference room), and a family room (which two of us set up desks in). The apartment had old radiators and no air-conditioning. We needed some office space because we had a staff of four with plans to get to eight quickly. (Our revenue was $1,9 million in year 3, so you can see we had a little bit of money to get an "office.")

Year 4: I rented the adjoining two-bedroom apartment, meaning I had two two-bedroom apartments. We had our first eight employees in that space. Let me just finish this part of our evolution by saying, in retrospect, the apartments were sort of awful. The heat was by radiator, which was really hard to get a consistent, comfortable heat. In the winter, you were either boiling hot or quite cold. In the summer, we had to go out and buy window air-conditioning units because there was no central air-conditioning or ceiling fans. And finally, the small kitchens and bathrooms, were, well, sort of gross. *But* it was home, it was easy to get/rent, and in a weird way, we all sort of loved those early days of grinding it out. (Our revenue was $3.5 million in year 4, so it was a good time to get some proper office space.)

Year 5: I rented our first commercial space. We did a sublease for one-third of the market price. We bought IKEA desks and equipment, and every new employee had to put together their own desk as a sort of initiation. The floor space was open, with nothing in it, so we were able to play legitimate games of boccie ball when we needed a break. It was sparse, but it was a class-A office space and was the right measure for where we were in our growth. (Our revenue was over $5 million in that year, and we grew to about a dozen people.)

Year 6: Our first real, true space that we leased and furnished. We were in business for over six years before we really spent any time finding space. At that time, we had roughly twenty to twenty-five employees, we had $9 million in revenue and were growing, and we were really a legitimate enterprise. We were so legitimate that we sold the business to a larger company that year (with an annual revenue approaching $10 million and about twenty-five people).

Key takeaway: We were very careful to not spend time hoping for sales leads and also not confusing time-sucking activities (like looking for office space) with results. We knew that if we grew the business, everything else would fall into place at the right time. We tried to be fully accountable for succeeding and would never have surrendered to the context.

Law 10—Providing Written Business Proposals: Dos and Don'ts

If you email a proposal that was not asked for, you can expect either a pretty quick no or a prolonged no-answer (silence).

Once again, there are books, courses, college degrees, seminars, and businesses based solely on making and closing sales. I am not trying to cover that broad terrain and boil the ocean on this one! That said, my main goal on this law is to share some real-life learnings and thoughts on providing written business proposals. As you will see in what follows, we spend a lot of time here, because this is a very important part of your success.

For the sake of clarity, written business proposals are serious documents. The written business proposal typically comes at a stage where the prospect truly understands the service/product, the costs, and the process to buy and how to implement what they have agreed to buy. They are in the know on what they are buying and, generally speaking, have asked all the key questions in your meetings and received satisfactory answers. As you will also see in the "one question *not* to ask" section, they have more than likely asked for a written proposal. A written proposal (contract) is not an email or the last few slides of a PowerPoint deck on which you outlined the costs and process. You may have used those to get clarity on the path forward, but they are not what I am referring to here.

Written proposals typically have a signature line for someone to take out a pen and commit themselves/their company to. We've all signed documents in our lives and businesses and know when something is serious. Some examples of written proposals would be letters of intent, statements of work (SOW), scope of services, and contracts. While there are a myriad of derivatives of those four documents, the general theme is that the documents are serious and enforceable.

Let's set the stage. You have worked hard to refine your product/ service/offering for a sale and have had a number of meetings with a prospect. You have worn your best business duds and are ready to close the sale (as they say) with a decision maker. All this sounds easy, but if have read the book to this point, you know it was tough. But the good news is, you're ready to sign up some business and make some hard-earned money. On the surface, the fact that you are providing a written proposal for contracting business is a good thing. Most of the time it is, but what follows is some advice on some dos and don'ts, and some lessons learned.

MAKING A WRITTEN PROPOSAL: THE DOs

Provide options: be ready with, and if possible, offer options in the contract. When providing a written proposal, offer some options so that the prospect can craft or tweak the path forward. Maybe it is an option A, B, and C, each with a distinct set of characteristics. By providing options in the proposal, you protect yourself from a hard no by giving the prospect ways to say yes. Put the prospect in the position to have some choices, which I will outline in a moment. Conversely (and not recommended), don't just give them one path forward or limited or no options in a written

> In my experience, a black-and-white one-size-fits-all proposal can be a template for not getting the deal.

proposal. In my experience, a black-and-white one-size-fits-all proposal can be a template for not getting the deal. I have gotten nos on proposals that were too hard coded only to find out later that if I had only offered things like more time to implement, a different payment schedule, or the options to include/exclude certain aspects of the work, I would have gotten the work.

Some of the options, or toggle switches, that I have found work well in proposals are the following:

- Project/product scope: For many services, there are baseline (no-frills), standard, and premium types of solutions. These variations of services or products provide a prospect a menu, per se, of ways they can move forward. Offering these in your proposal, or highlighting the one you feel meets the needs (with the others in the appendix), provides a feeling of flexibility to prospects. One size rarely fits all.

- Delivery or implementation timing: During the sales process, you may have heard there are better/worse times to deliver the solution. You may have heard timelines the prospect has. Is this a rush, or do you have time? The speed and date you deliver are nice options for a prospect to choose from.

- Term of the contract: If you have the ability to offer a few different terms, that could be a positive choice for the prospect. Can you offer a six-month, one-year, and even a multiyear term? Is this one and done, or are there ways/ options to continue to work and help the client?

- Price: This option is the one that you will probably want the least attention on, but the prospect (or their purchasing department—more on that later) will place the most attention on it. That is why I like to have an option or two for pricing, not only to show flexibility, but also steer a set of expectations on how "I" will flex in this area. The ways to option pricing are endless, but here are a few.

1. To think about pricing at a high level, the tried-and-true adage to express to a prospect is this: you can have any two of the following three things, but you cannot dictate them all: a) speed, b) quality, or c) price. A prospect can pick any two, but that means you pick the third. If a prospect wants something fast and of the highest quality, well then, you determine the price. If the prospect wants a low price and high quality, then you get to deliver on your terms (maybe when things are slow for you). You get it.

2. Baseline price and premium price. My experience is that the client typically ends up in the middle, and that is good. Nobody wants the minimum, but it is always good to show the floor below which you will not engage. There is nothing wrong with (in fact, I advise) setting a minimum. At any level lower than that, it is just not fair to you to make the efforts or sell the product. Call it your walk-away position. We moved our selling floor up over the years in one of my businesses, and in the last few years, we came up with: "We won't get out of bed for less than $50,000." We never expressed that to a client, but we knew internally that was our minimum. In the early days, it was more like $5,000. The premium price is where all the bells and whistles are, and where you have the ability to add in or take things out. I have also found clients rarely go for the premium price but will take components from that category and try to get them for a reduced amount.

3. Be aware of what currency you are dealing in. In a number of companies I am an investor in, we are constantly dealing with multiple currencies and the exchange rates, which can fluctuate wildly. If you do find yourself dealing in other currencies, I would advise you to seek advice and help from a professional who makes sure what you are doing is fair to you.

- Speed: How quickly does the prospect need the service/product? The faster and more dedicated the focus for delivery is, the more premium the price. If they are more flexible on speed, you can work to synchronize when it might be better for your company to deliver.

- Payment terms: How and when can the prospect pay for the services? I have had instances where a prospect offered to pay the entire contract price in advance but wanted a discount for that (which was fair). Some clients might rush to get the contract into a financial closing period (before year end). I have had times where a prospect needed me to straddle the bill between two fiscal years (pay half this year in December and the other half in January of the next year). Being flexible with payment terms can be a powerful option for both you and clients, and it pays (pun intended) to know what their thinking and needs are.

- Place: Is this a local deal (not a lot of travel or logistics), a domestic deal requiring travel and accommodations, or an international deal? The complexity of the delivery/implementation place can also have an impact on the terms and is an added toggle switch. Will you be able to come to the site once to do the project, or will you have to come there innumerable times?

- Warranty/follow-ups: What are the prospect's expectations or needs in terms of warrantying the work or the follow-ups needed? An example of this in one of my businesses involved the number of times we were expected visit a client who required flights and overnight stays to review our reports with their employees. If a client wants a one-and-done review, versus needing to have us make four to five separate, distinct presentations, it would play a factor/toggle in the written terms of the deal.

- Et cetera: There are potentially limitless options for clients, especially given the type of business you are starting. Listening to why the client wants to work with you, what they are going to use the product/service for, and how they have worked with other similar things in the past can guide you on the options you may want to consider.

A word of caution about options: While I outlined a lot of options and things to think about in the preceding section, try not to go overboard and overcomplicate the proposal. Taken to an extreme, you could end up providing so many options that the prospect gets more frustrated than feeling empowered. You should know going into a written proposal ideally what you want, and what you think the prospect will want. Try to craft options that are focused on *getting the deal closed* in a timely manner for each of you.

> Try to craft options that are focused on *getting the deal closed* in a timely manner for each of you.

Also, watch out for clients who keep adding, changing, and

deleting options over a prolonged period of time. A little zigzagging between proposals, options, and the signed contract is OK, but too much time can be a warning sign. When things get prolonged, I found it best to look for the simplest components of the deal so that I could just get started. Said another way, watch out for the clients who seem to be just playing at business and window shopping—and potentially wasting your time.

Lastly, be forewarned that some savvy buyers (or their purchasing departments) may try and structure the deal in such a way that they cherry-pick all of the best components of different options, thereby making the deal a bad one. If certain options only belong to certain solutions, be clear about that. For example, you can only provide a six-week delivery for the premium price. A prospect cannot take the six-week delivery and combine it with the lower-priced option. I have found that when confronted with an impossible (unprofitable) "ask" from a buyer during negotiations, it is OK to just say, "I'm sorry; I can't do that." If pushed for more, I would add, "It's not fair to what other clients of mine have paid" or "I do not make any margin on this, and that is not fair" or "If those are the terms, then maybe this solution/service/product is the wrong fit." Turn the tables back on negotiations that are not fair, and don't let someone cherry-pick options that make it a bad deal.

Make proposals in person. Try to never, ever send a written proposal in an email. I have found using email for proposals that have not been agreed to generally either get delayed and not acted upon, and having a prospect use email is an easy way for them to say no!

At the end of the meeting, where there is agreement about the client wanting a proposal (see the one question to *not* ask at the end of a sales meeting at the end of this law), set a time and date, right there in the meeting, to come back and walk through the proposal in person. If you have momentum for them wanting a written proposal, convert that momentum into the meeting to review the written proposal—in person (or via Skype/Zoom or other remote meeting technologies if needed)!

It's as easy as this: "Hey, I can come back before your workday gets started, or late in the day any day next week to walk you through the proposal?" Make it easy for them to meet with you. This is also a great closing/validation technique. If the client agrees to have you back in, that is a good sign for the sale and the need/urgency.

If the client says, "Just send me the proposal in an email" after you have asked to see them, I proffer that is not a good sign (usually). There are occasions where the client is rushing to make a decision, and that can be good, but generally speaking, when a client will not make time to see you to review a proposal, that can be a sign of low interest. I always read that as them just wanting to get me out of their office by asking for a proposal that they may have no intention of signing.

So what do you do? Am I wholeheartedly recommending never sending a written proposal in email? Well, yes, in a way. If a prospect will not budge after you try the following things, then, well, yes, you have to send it in email But, by trying the following tactics/ responses, I hope they will make the time, or you will "see" that the proposal was never really wanted:

- "From my experience in other companies, an in-person review is the best way to make sure I clearly review the contract and the options, and also hear any issues we need to address directly from you."

- "We put a lot of effort and work into our proposals, and I would appreciate the courtesy of reviewing it with you in person."

- "I have found that sometimes things can get a little lost in translation or confusing in the proposals, and for both our sakes, it would be better to talk it through together."

- "My company does not allow proposals to be emailed. We can email final/working contracts, but not proposals."

There are polite ways of trying to get in-person meetings with clients. You have to pick your own style and voice to express them, but I caution you to be ready for any pushback.

Email or nothing: What do you do when a client is firm, and they say, "Send me the proposal in email (or forget it)"? While you certainly have the option of saying no, I have never done that, nor do I recommend it. By saying no, you are taking what has probably been a positive set of meetings with the prospect and turning it into a test of wills. Instead, I recommend you acquiesce to the prospect's demand for email and offer the following tactics/ideas for you to consider:

- Be *fast*. For me, speed shows seriousness. I'd get them the proposal that day or first thing in the morning.

- Make the email time stamp (when it was sent) count. I would send it either very late at night (10:00 p.m. or later) or very early in the morning (before 6:30 a.m.). I want the prospect to see the email time stamp on it and see I stayed up late or got up extra-early to get that to them. I want to try and build gratefulness or at least respect from the prospect with my speed and attention to their request. I want them saying: "Wow, that was fast ... and look at the time of day they did it. It must be important to them!"

- By all means, put the price and scope in the subject line. Don't bury the important facts in the body of the email, the document, and the proposal you attach. This is business, so there is no need to be shy about quoting the scope and price.

- Mark it confidential. Once again, seriousness—and you also should protect your intellectual property. Often in written proposals, there is a wealth of proprietary items, and you do not want them forwarded around a company, industry, or competition. Put them on polite warning that it is for their eyes only.

- Follow up and send a hard copy overnight. Sending the written proposal in email does not mean you should leave it at that. Send *two* signed copies of the proposal in overnight mail (FedEx, UPS, et cetera) to the person. Include a hand-written note and the proposal signed by you, marked confidential. You need to a) show them you are serious, and b) make it easy for them to move forward. This helps to reinforce that you felt you had a closed deal with them.

- Put the features and benefits of the proposal in bold in the email. Stay focused on the client's needs, and keep high-lighting what your company does and how it maps to those needs. This is called features and benefits. We tend to focus on the features of our solutions, and while that is important, prospects buy for the benefits of what our solution does. Here is a trick to remembering this turn of phrase: every time you say something about your solution, put the words *which means* at the end of that statement. That forces you to state the benefits. Here are a few general, simple examples to describe this sales technique:

1. "I go to the gym to work out, *which means* I stay healthy" (the benefit of going to the gym is to be healthy).

2. "We do our work quickly, *which means* you will have the results you need by the next quarter" (the benefit is getting the stuff they need by the next quarter).

3. "We can be flexible on the scope, *which means* we can come in on budget" (the benefit is you are going to hit their budget amount).

So there you have it. That's a lot to digest when it comes to written proposals. As discussed, I spent more time than usual in this law because I have had so many experiences, good and bad, that I wanted to share. Also, this is an important moment in an entrepreneur's success because it generates you money, and as such, it warrants time, attention, and detail.

THE MAGIC QUESTION TO ASK AT THE END OF EVERY SALES MEETING

"This all sounds quite positive, but let me ask you, is there anything that you foresee happening that would stop you from signing a contract to move forward?"

Once you ask this, listen, shut up, and don't interrupt.

I cannot tell you how many times I thought I had a sale closed, followed up the meeting with a written proposal, and then either heard there were additional steps that needed to be taken (e.g., more meetings) or worse, I heard nothing back from them—utter silence.

It's human nature to want to leave a good sales meeting on a high note. We have all been coached: "When a deal is closed, or things went well, leave on a high note." But the fact is, sometimes sales are not as far along or as closed as we might like. Sometimes there were two to three more steps to the sales process that you may be unaware of if you don't ask the magic question. Sometimes there was competition. Other times there were issues of which, had I only used the magic question, I would have been so much better informed. Conversely, by not knowing that I should ask the magic question above, which is really about looking for obstacles or hidden/unrevealed next steps, I found out the hard way that I had not yet closed a sale, or the meeting was not as good as I thought it was.

> The more informed I was, the better I got at closing business and also timing when business would or might close.

Once I started asking the magic question, I came away so much better informed. The more informed I was, the better I got at closing business and also timing when business would or might close. I also got better at realizing when I might never close a business deal, which is sometimes just as important as knowing the good deals. Here are some examples of what I heard when I started asking the magic question:

- "Oh, I can't sign this contract. It has to be signed two levels up from me."

- "We are just at the beginning phase of even considering something like this at my company/department. We expect this to take months."

- "We are looking at three other vendors for this … and two are really strong. In fact, our purchasing department will be handling this after I qualify the vendors."

- "I'm moving to another department next week, and you will have to wait for my replacement to start up. It will be months before we act on this."

- "We just had total budget shutdowns for the balance of the year."

But hold on a minute—the answers to the magic question are not always bad. I don't want to make you so paranoid you don't want to ask it, as the magic question is designed to provide you information to get more deals done. So let me provide some bright spots:

- "I need a week to review this proposal and will then decide. I am presenting the solutions in an internal meeting next Friday and will have next steps then."

- "Nothing can inhibit this from happening, based on everything I have seen. I have the signing authority for this, and it can be implemented within my team."

- "My manager just told me we need to make this happen with you ... fast."

When you ask the magic question, you have to truly shut up and listen to the answers. Let the prospect talk, and resist the hesitation to immediately jump in to handle every objection. By not interrupting, you will get a clear view of the closing runway and how to land there (or realize you were nowhere near the airport yet).

If you do get an objection or two you can handle, then certainly handle it after they have spoken and finished. If, though, you get an avalanche of stuff or a deal breaker you did not see coming, it may be best to ask for another meeting to be scheduled (while you are still there) so you can come back in a few days. That will give you some time and perspective to come back with answers and options.

THE MAGIC QUESTION TO NEVER ASK AT THE END OF A SALES MEETING

"Can I send you a proposal?"

I believe a sales prospect has to *ask you* for a proposal. You should not offer it unsolicited. By simply asking, "What are the next steps?" and listening, you will see where you are in the sales/closing cycle, and you can see if they ask you for a proposal.

Unsolicited proposals are a waste of time and paper, and they create a mirage of imminent business. The easiest answer for a prospect to provide when asked about being sent a proposal is "Sure." The problem is, aside from the rare client who might say no and be honest with you, prospective clients will generally always say yes—"Sure, send me a proposal." In many cases, the reality is that many of them are just being nice and finding a cordial way to end a meeting. You take the yes as a closed sale, and they take the yes as "meeting over."

Try asking, "What are the next steps?" and/or the magic question ("Is there anything that would inhibit … ") as the closer. Clients should ask for a proposal and be somewhat interested and serious. There is nothing wrong with you stating that you put a lot of energy into a proposal and would be delighted to present them with one in person. You just want to make sure that is what they want. Don't get me wrong. You want to be making good proposals and "eating what you kill," but you don't need to waste time and satiate your hunger with too much false hope.

In closing, unsolicited proposals and sending proposals in email are *death*. Conversely, having a proposal *be* asked for, asking the magic question, and presenting a proposal in person are *life*. Stick to the latter, and you will find great success.

A word of caution about purchasing departments: In many of

the businesses I have been in, the client/company will often have a purchasing department. This is typical in large, multinational companies where billions of dollars are spent. That department is typically in charge of negotiating some or all large contracts for the company. In these instances, once a buyer decided to purchase our services, we were "thrown" to the purchasing folks to iron out the terms (price, length of contract, et cetera) with them. This is the equivalent of your general practice doctor saying they think you are OK, but they want you to see a proctologist, just in case. Ouch … and beware.

Once again, there are books, courses, degrees, and certificates on learning the art and science of purchasing (procurement, logistics, and so on). and I will not try and boil the ocean here. Instead, I will share some highlights to help educate you and make you aware of this critical step in getting a contract signed.

Purchasing departments, by their charters/mandates, are responsible for getting the best deals they can for their company. In my experience, while they will feign wanting a partnership, wanting to work together, and wanting to make a fair deal, they are measured on their before and after. Their before is: What were the terms of the proposal before they got involved? Their after is: What were the terms of the proposal after they got involved? Their *win* is the difference: What did they save, or what more did they get?

The trick to creating a win-win is to know this is going on and to play the game well. Here is some advice:

- Do not be adversarial. Be friendly and professional, but don't be tricked into thinking you're on the same team. You are not. You are probably not having beers with these folks any time soon (although we did, once, have a purchasing group take us out to dinner after a contract negotiation in Paris with a French pharmaceutical company!). You will see these folks only when there is money at stake and there are contracts in play.

- Understand the power your buyer has versus the purchasing department's power. Can the buyer sign the contract, no matter what the outcome? Or can purchasing put a kibosh on the deal or bring in competition if they are not satisfied? I have had instances where the buyer just needed me to meet with purchasing and, in fact, coached me to offer a 3 percent discount, and I would be fine. I have had instances in which purchasing was so tough they convinced the buyer to do an RFP (request for pricing/proposal) and ostensibly restarted the whole selling process to the beginning. It will run the range of possibilities, so know what power each party has.

- If you can create a helpful win for the purchasing department that does not cost you too much, it might be worth it. I have thrown the purchasing folks an occasional discount, sometimes better payment terms, and offered an added service period. Try to know what might make them look good, and you might be able to create some easy wins and keep things on track.

- When you think the deal and negotiation are done, they may come back and ask for just a tad more. They are going to play on your happy emotions about the deal being done and may come back and ask for a few more percent points off the price, or fifteen months of services for twelve months, or the ability to pay in ninety days versus thirty). Either way, be ready to offer a tad more, or respond by saying, "I appreciate you asking, but I have done all that I can."

- *All* of the toggles/options I reviewed in the beginning of this law also apply to dealing with purchasing. When they ask for something, you also get to ask for something. As I have outlined, this is all they do for a living, so don't be afraid to ask for things, as asking is a two-way street!

I will leave it at that and will just assert—be aware if this is coming. If it is, you may want to leave some dry powder (some givebacks and options) for this part of the negotiation and may not want to give it all to the actual buyer/user of your services.

LESSONS LEARNED

Sending Unsolicited Proposals Is a Losers' Game

After reading Law 10, you can almost guess I learned a lot of hard lessons with respect to closing business and written proposals. Luckily, I guess I had enough prospects to make it through those losing situations and also the resilience to keep going. That said, the lessons were really tough, but they created the learning experiences I have been sharing.

In the early days, I ended almost every good sales meeting by asking: "So can I get you a proposal?" As no surprise, in hindsight, just about everyone said, "Sure, email me a proposal." I thought I was on fire in terms of getting and closing business in those early days! If you read the companion to this book (*The Diary of Year One*, which is on my website as a free download at www.stephenegerard.com), you will see my naive enthusiasm for the amount of business (via unsolicited proposals) I thought had coming in ... but I did not. *The Diary of Year One* was a weekly handwritten diary I kept and wrote in each week to keep track of what was happening. It was also a cheap form of self-therapy, as I had some quiet time to celebrate and bemoan the successes and failures of the week in writing.

Key takeaway: Check out *The Diary of Year One* on my website at www.stephenegerard.com. I have been told it is an easy read, and it will reinforce some of the things I have outlined in this law, especially in the first few months.

Law 11—Knowing You're onto Something: Three Is the Magic Number

Getting one client is easy and potentially an anomaly. Getting the second client is the start of a trend. But getting the third one is the trick. Once you have your third client, you might actually be onto something!

Law 11 has nothing to do with the fabled "things come in threes" rule of life. While I did grow up in an Italian household where this was oft quoted, Law 11 comes from start-up experiences over multiple businesses … over multiple decades! This law is also not a one-size-fits-all law, as you may find it is your tenth client that got you over the hump, a revenue goal, or something else that had you feel like you were going to win. For me, it was and has been three clients that make a milestone.

First, don't get me wrong here. Closing business and getting the first one or two clients are worthy of a huge smile, a taste of champagne, and some soft high fives. I also don't want to be overly sarcastic in not recognizing some hard-earned success. In sales parlance, you have gotten the small segment of prospects who either like to be early adopters (clients who like to try new things and be on the leading edge) or a prospect that had a genuine need for what you are

> Now, more than ever, is the time to double down and focus on sales efforts and show that you can blow it out of the water by loading up the sales pipeline and closing more deals.

offering, right at that moment. Once again, that is good, but there is still more left to do.

Champagne and caviar dreams aside, I have seen too many people get caught up in the preliminary validation of getting one or two clients, and in the process, they lose sight of the need and urgency to get many more clients to have a sustainable business. In that, the tendency can be to let up on the gas or divert attention to other things in the business, like expanding capacity or looking for office space.

I would assert that now, more than ever, is the time to double down and focus on sales efforts and show that you can blow it out of the water by loading up the sales pipeline and closing more deals. Here are a few ideas to use on clients 1 and 2 to help you accelerate:

- Ask clients 1 and 2 for referrals. If they like what you are offering, they may know others who might also like it. Look them up on LinkedIn, and see if they are connected or even worked at other sales targets you may have. Professionals often jump around a bit within an industry, and they might be one or two degrees separated from a person or company you are trying to get into.

- See if these same clients have any networks in industry associations, trade groups, or other industry contacts. Early on, I was able to get a speaking engagement to expose hundreds of potential customers to our offering because one of my clients was the president of the industry trade group. I got lucky, as they needed to get speakers lined up for an upcoming industry conference.

- See if you might be able to do a press release on getting your first few clients. For this you might have to make the clients anonymous if they do not want to be named, but in any case, some good PR goes a long way.

- Do a check-in email and street mail updating your sales prospect base that you are off and running with some marquee clients. Make some noise, and create some FOMO (fear of missing out).

Keep evolving your offering and listening. There have also been instances where you can get so caught up and proud of the offering because two companies bought it that you close your ears and do not evolve the product/service further. It is easy to make excuses if the next few companies do not buy it by saying, "They missed the boat on what clients 1 and 2 saw in our product or service. It does not need changing. It was them!" Go back and reread Law 4. At this still early stage, you must still be adapting the solution and getting the next clients signed on. At this early stage of entrepreneurship, I would assert that your solution/service/product is nowhere near done and is not perfect. Keep evolving the offering based on feedback you are getting, and keep advancing it. Now, don't adapt it so much that clients 1 and 2 would not recognize it. Any adaptations would ideally have clients 1 and #2 saying, "Hey, you added some good things here."

Law 11 is not meant to be absolutely literal by identifying client 3 as your success point. The success-point client will be more of a feeling in that you intuitively know you're onto something. For your type of business, it could be when you have a certain percentage of the market or have a dozen clients. Trust me when I assert that you will know when you're on it! Remember, it's still very early in the business, and this law is about knowing when you have something and when you don't. Said another way, what this law is really about is distinguishing some early wins from the sustainable/telling wins. If you are a sharp entrepreneur, you will get a sense of what the markers and metrics are (clients, revenue, momentum) and will know you have graduated from the "Maybe this is going to work" phase to the "Whew, this is going to work" phase.

Beware of false metrics that could lead you to believe you are over the hump when, in fact, you are not. I have seen some entrepreneurs celebrate victory too early by focusing on the wrong metrics or holding the bar too low. Additionally, I have seen failures or missteps happen by confusing an activity with the desired result. Here are some gut-wrenching examples I have participated in, observed, and been close to. Even today, they make me cringe. These are the things I have sometimes been guilty of saying and have heard entrepreneurs say as a signal that they had made it … when in fact they had not made it quite yet:

- "We have three rounds of capital-raises done, and are heading into a fourth." While I know some business start-ups are capital intensive, raising capital is not an achievement in my eyes. It is an activity designed to get you moving toward achievements. Typically the business development (BD) people and venture capital folks raise this as "proof" of their success all the time. This may be their success metric, but it is not a success metric for the business. All this statement says to me is that the business is not profitable and is burning through money. I am well aware of the size and scale required to launch disruptive companies like Uber, Netflix, and so forth and the capital required to do that. My point is to make sure you never confuse the activity of raising money with the activity of launching a successful business.

- "Let me show you our marquee investors." Same as above— big deal! A lot of smart, marquee people occasionally make bad investments. Smart investors do not equal clients, revenue, and a sustainable business. I have also seen plenty of smart people invest in failed business ... and I have done so a few times in my life! Who invests in your business is not a guarantee of success.

- "We are speaking at the next *X* conference." Once again, this is an activity and not a result. It is probably an important activity and a good effort, but unless the business model makes its money off conference speaking, this is just a marketing activity. It's like saying, "We bought advertising in the *New York Times* or on Google."

- "Look at who we just hired." This one really frosts me (makes me cringe). This is typically a big-titled person either in the industry, in government, or in some relevant field that has been hired by the company. It is easy to make the mistake that this is a validator that the service/product is amazing. To me—and I'm being overly critical here—is that the person they just hired either needed/wanted a job, was tired of what they were doing before this, or maybe they wanted to coast for one or two more years before retiring. Hiring a "name" is just that: hiring a name. They may be a believer in the business and be a great addition to the team, but you still need to get paying clients and revenue.

- "We just leased ten thousand square feet of prime office space ... with an espresso machine." Well, you know how to spend money! Do you know how to make it?

My point in the examples above is to beware of false metrics. I recognize that I took my sarcasm to a new level in these examples and would have to confess to having learned all of these lessons the hard way, especially during my time in internet 1.0 (1998–2001), when the internet was born … and then crashed. I was attracted by companies that spoke this way, and I was guilty of speaking that way also. Lessons learned and sarcasm applied.

LESSONS LEARNED: SUCCESS AND FAILURE

A Story of Success: Three Is the Magic Number!

The benchmarking business (TGaS Advisors) I started was reliant on getting five similarly sized pharmaceutical companies to simultaneously provide us information. That information would allow us to compare each of them to each other, using us as the intermediary. It was no easy feat getting five clients at one time but was something worth trying. Getting our first two clients was quick. Each of those companies was led by executives that I had personally known for more than fifteen years. They were old friends and colleagues and trusted that I had a good idea and could get the five clients I needed to start the business. Each of them threw me a bone and joined within months of starting the business. So we had clients 1 and 2 out of the five we needed.

I set that context to take you through the story and the revelation that client 3 was our milestone client.

While I could have looked at getting clients 1 and 2 as success metrics, I could not really in good conscience tally them as solid scores. While they felt I had a good idea and were enthusiastic supporters, I knew I needed to sign up clients who had never met me before or new clients who owed me nothing.

Getting the third client (this is a repeat from Law 6—Fail Fast and Fail Forward) was going to be a validator for me. As you can reread in the Lessons Learned in Law 6, I was able to convince Procter & Gamble pharmaceuticals to join after they originally said no, making them client 3. They were a milestone for me because I did not know them and was able to convince them to join after receiving a no—hence Law 11: there are milestones and clients, and you will know them when you get them or pass them.

Since our business model was based on getting five clients, there was little time to celebrate client 3. We eventually went on to get our fourth and fifth clients in the subsequent months and were off and running. Client 4 came through a referral, but I had never met him, so it was another good validator. Client 5 came through another fifteen-plus-year pharma colleague, so while it rounded out the needed five clients, it was not a validator metric. Out of our first five clients, three of them knew me quite well, but two of them I had never met.

Beware of False Metrics—One Client Does Not a Business Make!

It was the internet 1.0 era (1998–2001), when the internet was just coming of age. You could not pick up a business publication without reading that the future has arrived and that the future was the internet. The early pioneers from those days were companies like AOL ("You've got mail"), Google (a crude web search engine), Amazon (a book seller), and Netscape (a web browser).

In 2000, after fifteen years with large *Fortune* 50 companies, I went to work for an early internet darling, DrKoop.com. DrKoop.com was a healthcare website, the initial model of which was based on providing authoritative medical and pharmaceutical content to consumers, and then selling advertising and sponsorships to companies that wanted to grab those eyeballs. The targets for the advertising sponsors were going to be pharmaceutical companies as well as any healthcare products aimed at healthy living. An early competitor and pioneer, WebMD, is a good reference point, as it is still in business today and is quite well known.

Anyway, DrKoop.com had raised some $80 million to $90 million before I got there and was a leading company that was always in the press. By the time I got there, they had already gone through the bulk of the capital raise in deals with AOL and other internet partners. Based in Austin, Texas, it was up and running ... and running fast! These were the days of big company signs on the sides of beautiful office spaces, beanbag conference areas, snacks galore in the lunchroom, and dogs at work. Everyone had $600 Herman Miller chairs and modular cubicles ... the money was flowing.

I joined on to lead the pharmaceutical division and work to sell advertising and sponsorship packages to pharmaceutical companies. With my fifteen years of experience in the pharmaceutical industry, I was ideal for the position and ripe for the challenge. This was going to be my entrepreneurial baptism and my pathway to fame and fortune—or so I thought!

When I joined, they had just sold a diabetes sponsorship to a pharmaceutical client in the mid-six-figures—a nice deal. When I got there to run the division, they were in full celebration mode for months, based on getting one deal. While I was, of course, pleased with the deal and also bolstered by that success, I knew we needed to get ten times more deals of that size or larger to hit our goals (and pay the bills).

What we/I did not realize—and to the learning that three is the magic number when it comes to clients—was that our first client was a mirage, as we were about to find out. It turns out that we had gotten an early adopter at a pharmaceutical company who had a real passion/vision for early internet 1.0. Their exuberance for being with the in crowd and tying up a sponsorship deal in the diabetes area, on the surface, looked good. As we progressed, though, it became apparent that the buyer had overextended themselves and did not have the authority to do a deal of that size. The contracted amount was far more than they could sign up for at their authority level. From our side, it also carried with it an advertising commitment (eyeballs and clicks) that would be impossible to achieve. We had sold something we could not really deliver to someone who did not have the authority to actually buy it. We had created a mirage in the desert, and it took us months to realize it, and by then, it was too late.

Key takeaway: For months we held up that one client as the validator for everything that was to come. We—led by me, admittedly—went out and priced everything we had even higher than that first mirage sale. We were also much more cocky and aggressive in everything we did with that one client in hand. From that one deal (versus getting three clients), we wasted time and money trying to replicate it and exceed it, when we should have just been modest and gotten a few more lesser clients. A few more clients would have created some momentum and real confidence. Instead, that one client sank us in terms of our division getting any real traction. That coincided with the crash of internet 1.0 in the spring of 2000.

PHASE IV—THE EMOTIONAL PHASE: RIDING THE ROLLER COASTER OF EMOTIONS

You'll be going through a roller coaster of emotions (daily), so knowing what to expect can help, knowing that you're not alone, and knowing when to recalibrate can be of comfort.

With good reason, I have spent most of the time on the first three phases of being becoming an entrepreneur. Let's face it: if you can get these phases right, you will have the best shot at being in business and having your definition of success. If you don't get that right, then more than likely, you will spend too much time in this phase … and that will be hard.

I will be a little more punchy and brief in this phase. This phase is not only provided to help you with expectations but also to provide you some relief in knowing you're not alone. Every entrepreneur worth their salt goes through these emotions, so take comfort in knowing no matter what the degree of success other entrepreneurs have that they have been here. This phase will also last until you are well over the hump (Phase V) and really have a truly sustainable business ... which probably will take a few years.

A quick word on my *tonality*: It may seem that the tone of this book, or at least the Emotional Phase, is one of sarcasm. That is not my goal, as *I am with you*, not against you. Aside from my form of expression being somewhat sarcastic, sprinkled with a gallows type of humor, please do not take it as negative. There are lessons to learn, and sometimes a little humor and sarcasm help along the way.

I have referenced *The Diary of Year One*, a free download on my website that will provide a real-life, weekly example of just how emotional and lonely things can get. During my first year in business, I kept a weekly diary to sort of help me reflect on the week that just passed, take a look back at prior weeks to look for trends and learning, and just give me some quiet time for "therapy." *The Diary of Year One* is not a book meant to scare you, but more to share what I learned with you and to let you know you are not alone (but you are on your own). If you read it, you will, in fact, see the exact moment and example of when I learned, discovered, or synthesized many of the phases and laws in this book.

Every true entrepreneur will experience all of these emotions, unless they have a trust fund and don't give a crap if it fails. The "emotions" give you a place to understand that it's OK to be feeling the way you do or might be. I also hope it provides you with fuel so that you don't get stuck in one or two of them. The emotions are mostly speed bumps along the entrepreneurial journey, and they should be treated and recognized as such. They are not car wrecks, although they may feel like them.

So let's jump in and show some emotions ...

Law 12—You Are on Your Own. And That's OK!

Never let success get to your head, and
never let failure get to your heart.

This law is about loneliness, whether actual or metaphorical. I would assert that being on your own is something you should actually relish! I did! Don't get me wrong, though. While it is scary, it really boils down to your own self-confidence. You have to believe in your own ability to succeed without any (or much) help. Don't confuse self-confidence with a brashness or cockiness. It is not. It is a self-confidence born out of the belief that you have the right ideas and the innate ability to adapt them and succeed with them. I believe that loneliness is self-confidence's fuel. Any feelings of loneliness should be fueled (positive visioning here) with positive thoughts that better and less-lonely days are coming.

> When the actual work and heavy lifting needs to start is when loneliness starts to set in.

One of the first times you will deal with this emotion is not on day 1 of your venture. Your day-1 decision to start a business is not rooted in loneliness. It is, in fact, rooted in excitement. Loneliness sets in on day 2 after you have decided to start your own business. When the proverbial office door closes, and you're left alone with the enormity of the task at hand ... that's when you will get lonely. When the actual work and heavy lifting needs to start is when loneliness starts to set in.

Remember that the world was not idly sitting around waiting for you to start your business. Your friends and family were not either. It's that harsh and yet that simple. Even if your business involves selling to family, friends, and former colleagues, you need to be thinking well beyond them in terms of sustainability and not using them to combat loneliness.

Loneliness is a feeling, not a physical thing. Even if you have business partners and/or employees, the determinant for success is yours and yours alone, hence the feeling of loneliness. I actually believe that most entrepreneurs are or were dying to be on their own and may even enjoy a little loneliness, or they would have never started the business. I am alone in writing this book—sitting in a library, hunkered in, alone and loving it.

In your desire to combat loneliness, be careful of the natural pivot (decision) to bring on partners, employees, contractors, or consultants. Stay lean and nimble. Even if you have taken investment money, stay lean, and stay focused on things I have already covered (getting revenue!). There can be a tendency to combat loneliness with detrimental activities. Don't fall into the combat-loneliness tactics of hiring other execs, giving away portions of your business to partners without performance criteria, spending too much time walking around Staples (I used to and still do this too much), or other things that are not about getting clients and advancing the business. Once you really get the business going, you will have more than enough time to combat the loneliness with other activities. In fact, when those things start taking your time and attention, you will long for the lonely, simpler days.

Words of caution on loneliness: Let's not take loneliness to an extreme and confuse that with being a hermit. In my first year, I thought it was important to have an office address and also people to bounce ideas off. To do that, I bartered a desk in a small advertising firm's office, which I have already written about. My point for resurfacing that is to reinforce that being alone is not 100 percent literal. You need to talk to people and refine your ideas. You need to network. You need to get referrals; you need to be out. While you are alone in owning that, you do not have to be alone in doing it.

Be wary of overextending yourself and hiring staff to combat the loneliness. My first four key "hires" were not salaried people, and they did not join until well into the first and second year of being in business. In fact, they were all revenue-sharing arrangements. I could not afford to pay people, so I found people that were willing to take a percentage of revenue, if we got any. This kept things lean, got me some company and collaborators, and kept me from being totally lonely.

LESSONS LEARNED

Dealing with Being Solo

Find a way to self-reflect on a frequent basis. While loneliness might imply quietness, they are different. I found I needed to create quiet time within the loneliness to reflect and pause. To do this, I sort of unwittingly kept a weekly diary during my first year in business. Every Friday, religiously, I would close the door in my home office or sit on the outside deck and write a few pages about the week that was. I would often look back a few weeks to see what I had written as a starting point for the week's diary entry. That diary became *The Diary of Year One*.

Truth be told, I am not a diary kind of guy. But I found the diary helped me think about the week, reflect on prior weeks, and also plan ahead. Since I was on my own and "lonely," it was a cheap form of therapy and almost an internal board meeting. It became a place I would vent a little if I needed, celebrate a bit when warranted, and panic to some extent ... all in private. I read the diary fairly frequently as a way of calibrating how it was going. I would reflect on what I said or wrote in prior weeks and see if those things happened, or did not, weeks or months later. I would be able to start to see patterns and "laws," many of which would become this book. Frankly, *The Diary of Year One* led to this book.

Finally, loneliness does not mean being a loner. I have mentioned that you need to make sure you have a few good people to bounce your ideas off. I cannot stress enough that my identification of loneliness is not a literal mandate to send you into monastic silence. Just understand, it can and will be lonely when you are out on your own ... and that's OK!

Key takeaway: As I described, early on, I made arrangements to have a desk at another start-up advertising agency in Princeton so that I had a) a place to go, b) some basic office stuff (internet, copier/fax, conference room, desk, phone), and c) some people to bounce ideas off. There were times I went into that office just to be around people, even if it was to listen and grab a coffee. Look for creative ways to network with people who can help your journey be better.

Law 13—Embarrassment and Pity: Your New Best Friends

You have to put in the drudgery. Every successful person started out at some point as a schlep.

—Helen Gurley Brown

When you put yourself out on a limb to start a business, you are out there and exposed for everyone to see. When you succeed, it is glorious. Conversely, when you stumble and have failures, it can be embarrassing, and at times you will find yourself being pitied. You know the old saying: "If this were easy, everyone would be doing it." Nobody signs up knowingly or wantonly for embarrassment and pity; they just come with the turf. It's that simple.

Regarding Law 13, I am going to run a little long-winded here in the Lessons Learned section. Why? 'Cause, man, I was embarrassed and pitied a lot in my first year or two. So no matter what you may read as the tone of my writing (sarcastic humor), please understand that I have been through all of these emotions (and laws), often numerous times. If I can save you from a few stumbles, or at least commiserate with you and let you know you have fellow solder-in-arms, well then, amen!

An entrepreneurial venture involves risk and a willingness to go past the edge of what seems typical. On the journey, you will lose some money (hopefully just initially), at times be embarrassed, and at times run the risk of being pitied. The embarrassment is more public and often happens when you are in the room. The pity—well, that's another thing altogether. Pity rarely happens when you are in the room but evidences itself in comments you hear later.

For all the bravado (quiet bravado and confidence, I hope) you get from starting a business, this is the blowback you get. You need to know it happens, know it is coming, and just give it a laugh.

Why will embarrassment and pity come your way, you may ask? There are times when you are going to have to ask for things that are uncomfortable ("Hey, I really need a favor"), which means you are going to get answers that can embarrass you. There are times where people may actually laugh and even scoff at your idea or business. The scoffing may even feel like pity ("Oh, man, good luck with that!" or "I know someone who tried something like that and failed"). Recognize that is going to happen. There are countless stories of almost every successful businessperson and their business being laughed at.

The last thing I will add before the stories: Embarrassment and pity should be treated as fuel for you. They are logs on the fire and will be secondary sources of fuel ("Man, I'll prove them wrong"). I say *secondary fuel* because your primary fuel should always be a belief that your ideas will attract clients and deliver you the success you are looking for. Instances of embarrassment and pity stoke the already-existing flames a little higher, or serve to rekindle some aspects of the desire that might be burning low.

I'm not quite saying "seek out embarrassment and pity" as much as I advise you that they are coming for you. Be ready.

LESSONS LEARNED

Man Down: Turtle on His Back in the Dead of Winter

I went to *The Diary of Year One* for this story, although it is vivid in my head, like it happened yesterday. If anyone wants to look up the date to verify the weather, I was in Connecticut on January 15, 2004, which was three weeks into me starting a business and the day before my forty-first birthday. It snowed four inches that morning, and was 0°F in Connecticut on that evening with a wind chill that made it feel like -20°F. The news said it was "the coldest night in a century," and I believe it!

I had traveled to New Jersey, then New York, and then lower Connecticut, from my home in Pennsylvania, for four distinct meetings in one day. I wanted to use my travel time as effectively as possible, so I stacked up a bunch of meetings. I boogied from meeting to meeting in the snow and the cold, and unfortunately, none of them bore any immediate fruit (sales). Read on ...

The first meeting was with a printing vendor that I had given a lot of business to (hundreds of thousands of dollars) when I was at a large pharmaceutical company. During that time, he was very early on in his business, so I was helping a fledgling entrepreneur in a big way. I felt he would be a great help to me, and I offered to do some consulting for him to help me pay the bills. I also felt he "owed" me some help, aside from the fact I thought I could provide him some good advice. Well, he did not see it that way and, in fact, pitched me helping him get more business for himself. I was there for a well-deserved favor, and it turns out *he* asked me for a favor! That was the first confounding and sort of embarrassing meeting for the day.

At the second meeting, I was pitching a paltry $7,500

consulting agreement with a company I had done some free advising for. I also thought they owed me a few shekels and a favor, but the person I was meeting with did not seem to see it that way. Not only was she not biting on the small consulting deal I was sort of pleading for, but she actually continued to seek free advice. It was another dose of embarrassment and head-scratching for me.

For the third meeting, I sped my car into New York City for a meeting in Manhattan with a potential pharmaceutical client. That meeting was abbreviated from a planned one hour to twenty minutes and did not bear any fruit. After all the tolls and parking fees, I hustled back across the George Washington Bridge to make my way to Connecticut. So, by the time I was getting to the fourth meeting, we can see my day was not going well at all.

The fourth meeting of my Arctic sojourn was a dinner meeting. I was having dinner that evening with an old colleague who was now with a top 20 pharmaceutical company. I really wanted to get them as a client. We had known each other ten-plus years and had done a decent amount of business with each other. We had a history and also enjoyed each other's company. He had ventured out on his own in Europe, and I tried on a few occasions to help him and even tried to hire him. So this was dinner with a fellow I also felt owed me some help ... and maybe even a sale!

Let's be polite and say the dinner went just OK. I was not feeling any energy or love from the meeting or the imminent chances for follow-ups. In fairness to him, he had just started with his new employer, and he needed to get his feet under his desk for a few months before recommending me. Fair enough, but waiting months for a recommendation was not what I was hoping for. Dinner sort of ended in a "meh!"

So, after driving three or four hours to get to New Jersey, New York, and Connecticut for what turned out to be a few marginal (shitty) meetings, I was feeling a little down. I clearly felt I was owed more consideration than maybe I had earned, and that had me bummed.

After the dinner and a very long day, I went out to my car in the *frigid* cold and drove to my *motel*. I emphasize motel because it was a $55-a-night place where the heater is under the window, the room doors open to the outside (not a hallway), and you get one towel with a bar of soap the size of a thin mint. That's all I could afford.

That's where a little of the embarrassment and self-pity crept in. Months before this, I was a well-paid senior vice president of a company, staying in the nicest hotels, being driven to sales calls by my sales team, and eating at some pretty nice restaurants. I had a corner office in Princeton, New Jersey, in a beautiful new office building and had sixty people working in my group. I was on top of the world.

Now I was an entrepreneurial slug, in the hinterlands of Connecticut, well off the highways and byways, in the freezing cold ... staying in motels. If embarrassment and pity were starting to creep in, they were about to come crashing down—literally. When I got out of my car to go into my motel room, I slipped on some ice by the trunk of my car and landed flat on my back. I had literally taken a header at 10:00 p.m. in the middle of a parking lot, on a sheet of ice, and I lay there like a turtle on his back.

I lay there stunned that I was lying on ice, on the ground, in -20°F weather. While I was not injured at all, I lay on the ground, eventually laughing at my predicament. My gallows humor kicked in. Oh, how the mighty had fallen (literally), and wasn't it funny? I was on my back in parking lot of a $55-a-night motel on the coldest day of the century, the day before my birthday. I was literally alone, embarrassed, and pitiful! Another person saw me and, after asking if I was OK, said, "It's tough being out on the road in sales, huh?" Now my plight was being parodied with *Death of a Salesman* humor.

As one final kick in the ass, and to add insult to injury, I could not get my motel room's heater (a window unit covered in black soot) to get the room's temperature above 55°F. It was a long day of crappy sales meetings, followed by an unactionable dinner, punctuated by an episode of Ice Capades in the parking lot, and a cold, uncomfortable night in the room.

If that does not bring a sense of embarrassment and pity to your soul, what will?

"Let Me Buy Your Lunch; You're Unemployed"

When I was in the Lunching Stage (see Law 5) of my first start-up, I went to grab a bite with an old colleague of mine. I felt he would be a good source of advice, a potential source of referrals, and just a good sounding board and someone to have on my side as I progressed. He had worked for me for a number of years, and we always had a good, collegial relationship. At a minimum, I was expecting some sound thinking and maybe a sales lead? Boy, was I wrong, because embarrassment and pity were about to join us for a bite!

From my side of the table, I was the brave soul, venturing out in the world with amazing ideas to start a business. I was someone to be maybe admired a bit ("Boy, I wish I was starting my own business!"). I was coming to lunch as a rising entrepreneur looking to stay connected to the working class (ha ha).

What became apparent quickly, though, was that from his side of the table, he saw me as a failure, per se. I had gone from the comfort and security (and success) of a big cushy job working together with him, to becoming a journeyman who was now onto his third new thing since leaving working with him years before. I think he may have come looking to see a cowering, half-beaten former colleague.

We had a cordial lunch with a few laughs about the past. But he gave me no help at all. He offered marginal feedback; there was no offer of referrals, and he almost seemed to want to eyeball me and scoff at what he deemed to be a low point in my career. So here we are, at lunch with two very different perspectives on what the situation was. From my side, I was on the rise, and from his side of the table, he was taking in how the mighty had fallen.

It all became crystal clear to me when bill for lunch came. I said I was going to pick up the tab since I had asked him out. His reply said it all: "Hey, let me get the lunch bill; after all, you are unemployed!"

Whaaaat? I was not unemployed (yet I was). I was creating a business, and that is different, right? There was pity, right in my face, and a sense of embarrassment for how it went down. I had gone from being this fellow's manager to someone he looked at as a failure.

That comment shaped a lot of how I went forward in trying to understand the potential mindset of people in meetings and how they would view me in the early days. While embarrassment and pity were strange bedfellows to me in the past, they were now my sidekicks. I would work to change that in the future, but for now, it was what it was.

Law 14—Highs and Lows and the In Betweens

It's never as good as it seems and not as bad as it gets.

Stay balanced; this, too, shall pass. This law is pretty straightforward. There will be days where you literally feel like you are on top of the world. There will also be days where you feel the weight of the world on you. It's OK! The key to living in this emotional law is knowing this is going to happen and using the quote above to maintain a sense of equilibrium. You could easily play with the quote to give it another angle ("It's never as good as it gets, and never as bad as it seems"). Take your pick. Either way, it is meant to convey a sense of the moment not being enduring, but in fact a passing one, and that you should not get too hung up on it.

Let's break it down into its two parts: *"It's never as good as it seems ... "*

This first half of the saying is designed to be a little cheeky by using "seems." The implication is that the good times are a bit of a point-in-time illusion. They are that mirage in the desert, and one should not get too overconfident when things seem to be going well. One should also not think that they will last forever. You will have days, even a few hours, where things are going great. Maybe a sale or two will happen that provide some nice revenue and good clients. Maybe an idea really crystallizes after spending time with it being foggy. The key in this emotional law is to know that this is a point in time to be celebrated, but not a trend line signaling that "this is always how it is going to be." Understand that it is a high; ride it, but know that it ends.

A good analogy for the surfers out there might be like riding a great wave. You have the ride of your life with a great takeoff, a couple of great turns and carves, and maybe some time in the "tube." Better yet, everyone on the beach and in the lineup saw it. You paddle back out to the hoots and hollers of your surf crew and settle in as the new Duke Kahanamoku of the break. That moment seems great, and in fact is "as good as it seems." Then, at that very moment of celebration, you see more waves, big ones, on the horizon. So let's jump to the second half of the saying and come back to our surfing analogy in a moment.

Let's break down the second part: *"and not as bad as it gets."*

Once again, I am being a little cheeky here. There will be what seems like weeks, days, and hours where you are taking a drubbing, and it feels awful. Knowing this is also a passing issue is always important to stay balanced. I used to actually take a bit of gallows humor in these moments and utter, "Well, you're really getting your ass kicked here." That humor, or whatever your own coping mechanism is, will help you weather these storm clouds.

Let's harken back to our surfer analogy from above. You know, the one where you rode the wave of your life to the cheers of the crew. Well, after you had the wave of your life (the "as good as it seems" moment), you paddle back out basking in your glory. You get set up for another epic ride because you're the new star in the surf lineup. At that moment, the horizon starts to blacken a bit with waves on the horizon—big ones! Everyone gets a bit of a knot in their stomach and says that little prayer that goes something like this: "Please, God, get me through this, and I will go to church." A huge three-wave (because they always come in three) cleanup set of waves rolls through and pounds you and your crew. The first wave, you barely scratch over, but you're OK. The problem is that you have used up a lot of energy and are out of breath, huffing and puffing. You frantically paddle toward the second wave, and it catches you as you paddle up the face, and it buries you backward over the falls. You spend a tumultuous fifteen seconds underwater like a rag doll, but it seems like a minute. And just as you come up, the third wave, the grand-daddy of them all, pounds you into the sand twelve feet below the surface. When you finally surface, you have sand everywhere. It's in your nose, your ears, and your mouth. The result of that three-wave set has you washed into the shore or the reef. When you finally catch your breath and thank God, and think it is all right, you realize your $750 surfboard has broken in half.

> Understand there are bad times, and know that they will end.

The point of my long-winded surfer analogy: Highs and lows are all within five minutes of each other. The great wave was fleeting, and the beatdown has passed. Your surfing session and ability are probably somewhere in between. Understand there are bad times, and know that they will end.

All that said, make sure to take away lessons during the good and bad times. Learn and refine what worked, and adapt to or throw out what did not. If you do that, you will naturally maximize the good times and minimize the bad. Learn to recognize these highs and lows, and enjoy both for what they offer you. Ride them, but don't for a minute believe either will last forever.

LESSONS LEARNED

Sir Ernest Shackleton: A Story of Highs and Lows and a Lot of Resilience (Law 16)

For this lesson, I pivot outside the business world to one of the most epic stories of managing the highs and lows of what you can be faced with. Books and movies have recounted this epic adventure, but I will use just a few paragraphs.

Sir Ernest Shackleton, with a full crew under his command, set out on a wooden sailboat from England to explore the Antarctic in 1914 and 1915. This had never been done before. He not only sailed to the Antarctic and crossed the Roaring Forties (the treacherous waters below Chile, South America), but he sets out to cross it from sea to sea with his crew aboard the ship *Endurance* (aptly named).

Being that this was a new grand adventure, I would imagine that the planning and the beginning of the trip sort of feels like the "never as good as it seems" part of the quote I have outlined. I imagine it was fun to tell people at cocktail parties, before he left, how epic the venture would be (in his own humble manner). As he set sail, he probably gave a good laugh at the poor schlubs living ordinary lives in England. My point is that there had to be some swagger and a feeling of "this seems good" in the air. At that moment, Sir Ernest has to think, in his own quiet way, that he is the *man*. I would proffer that is where the "good as it seems" starts to erode as they lose sight of the English shores and set sail for Antarctica.

Fast-forward to the "never as bad as it gets" portion of the quote. After months at sea, Sir Ernest and his crew make it to the Antarctic. Then, his boat literally gets stuck in the ice, squeezed like it's in a vise grip, with no prospect of getting out or being rescued. In fact, it gets so bad that his boat quickly starts to get destroyed by the encroaching ice.

Oh, it gets worse! He then sets out with a small group of his crew in a small—let me repeat, *small*—rowboat/sailboat to try and get help. He's in the Southern Ocean, the treacherous Roaring Forties, the most ferocious waters on the planet, in a small rowboat? He proceeds over the course of the next weeks to make it to remote Elephant Island, and then ultimately South Georgia Island. The journey takes him 720 nautical miles in freezing rain, with little food and water—in a rowboat!

Finally, on South Georgia Island, he finds himself on the mountainous side of the island, not on the side where there is a village. He then has to climb over the mountains to reach people and get help. He finally reaches help and then takes weeks to finally get back to his team, which was stranded with the ship. Adding insult to injury and context to this story, the team that was stranded with his sailboat in the freezing Antarctic had no idea, *no* idea, whether he had made it and was coming back for them.

Let me first say that I give Sir Ernest's incredible feat a real injustice recounting it in the way I do and with the brevity to which I lend it. That said, I use it to illuminate that there were amazing highs and lows for Sir Ernest and his crew. Many of them were matters of life or death. He had to have had a mental quality that provided him a way to endure the highs, power through the lows, and carry on.

Just like one starts a new business venture (which, by the way, is not life and death) and must endure the highs and lows and forge on, there is a lot to be learned from

Sir Ernest Shackleton. His moniker eventually became "Through endurance, we conquer."

Key takeaway: While that might not be the exact case for a new entrepreneurial venture, it is close. Recognize that the highs are fleeting, the lows will also pass, and it's the in betweens and your resolve to endure that matter.

Law 15—The Bermuda Triangle of Emotions: Balancing on the Head of a Pin

Knowing when to push hard, when to proceed with caution, and when to wait is tricky. Sometimes, believe it or not, no action (sleeping on it) is the best action.

Just like the fabled Bermuda Triangle, there is a business Bermuda Triangle to watch out for. This triangle is characterized by three competing mindsets. Once again, the trick is to understand when you are "in" the famed triangle, stay calm, and most importantly, know what to do.

The Bermuda Triangle of Emotions are: patience, persistence, and panic.

Imagine a triangular object balancing on the head of a pin. These three words are on each corner, looking like a floating compass or gyroscope on a boat. They are always in motion, swaying and gyrating, and always in need of some correction. That is what to expect in the early days, weeks, months, and years of starting a business. You will be continually balancing these three competing emotions.

Let's face it; there are infinite situations and examples that require balancing these emotions. I will provide a few in the stories in the Lessons Learned section, but in no way can I provide a definitive set of ways or actions for

> The greatest single piece of advice for navigating the triangle of emotions I can give you is to *sleep on it.*

every circumstance. My goal here is to acquaint you with this law and help you realize it exists. I will also try and articulate some general, measured actions. I also want to let you know it is going to be all right if you get caught in the triangle. Every entrepreneur has been twirled around in this triangle … and most get through it.

To decide the right triangulation, or action to take, for every instance you encounter, it will take trust in your judgment/gut. Additionally, you may want to try and get some perspectives from others ("Hey, what do you think about this situation? What would you do?"). The greatest single piece of advice for navigating the triangle of emotions I can give you is to *sleep on it*. I have almost always found a new perspective when I let something sit for about twelve hours and come back to it the next day. I have made better decisions and had better outcomes by taking a breath. That is not to say you should inactive and wait a day for every decision. It is more to say that when there are tough decisions with profound consequences, don't be afraid to sleep on it. Even when a person or client is trying to back you into it ("I gotta know today, or else"), sleep on it. Unless you are a heart surgeon, waiting a day never hurt anything.

Here is a quick example of the balancing act in the triangle of emotions:

You are dying to close a sale on a Monday (persistence), but you know Mondays are crappy days for closing sales. You know you should wait till Friday (patience) because Fridays are the best days for closing sales. You decide to wait! But then, Wednesday rolls around, and you're getting anxious, really anxious. You "panic" and go for it, trying to close the sale with an email. You *lose* the sale. In this small, simplified example, patience needed to win out (waiting until Friday), but panic won … and you lost.

PATIENCE

It is easy to confuse patience with inaction or being passive. They are not the same thing. Patience is taking a measured approach and having a plan. The plan could include waiting, with some minor actions, but waiting nonetheless and letting some things unfold. You can be patient and provide some time to make things happen.

A simple example of patience would be waiting for a yes or no decision on a sale from a prospect. Let's face it: when you are waiting for a yes or no decision on a sale from a prospect, an hour seems like a day, a day seems like a week, and a week seems like a month. But, through the eyes of the prospect, who is busy doing their job, they will get to the decision in due time. Their timeline is not your timeline. This is where some degree of patience is warranted. It will take some persistence (this is the next topic area), but that persistence may need to wait (patience).

There were times in the early days of my first business where I pinged (emailed) a prospect so much that they came back to me and said, "Chill out; I need some time." My impatience, in those instances, caused me to realize we were operating on different urgency schedules. I needed to sell something so I could eat (and stop withdrawing money from the bank), while they had a full-time job, were eating well, and would make a decision in due course. As my business grew and we had some breathing room, we could afford to be more patient, but in the early days, it was tough to be patient.

Calibrating your patience is situationally based. Measured, common sense should guide you on what a fair amount of time to be patient is and also what patience looks like. Try to walk around each situation, and look at it from your perspective as well as the other party's perspectives. Taking an honest, 360-degree view of a situation will help you measure the amount of patience to give it. Here are some variations of patience to chew on:

Do nothing. There are times where you should be totally silent. Just let it sit and wait. This is the toughest kind of patience because you may feel like you are not being aggressive. Do not confuse lack of aggressiveness with being too patient. You can be an aggressive businessperson yet know when to exert patience.

Do a little something. There are times to be patient, but as I like to say, ping the situation, or stir the drink. These are the "Hey, just checking in" or "Thought you would find this helpful in moving things along" types of outreach. They are not, though, the "What's your decision?" or "I thought I would have heard from you by now" outreaches. It might be the bump-into-them scenario you create, and keeping it light when you do. It can also be a reach-out that has nothing to do with business. Perhaps you both shared stories or interests on being baseball fans, as an example. Maybe it is an outreach like "How about that Yankee game last night?" It lets them know you are there but also does not stalk them.

Do something (showing impatience). There are times when you have been patient, maybe pinged the situation, and have now earned the right to be somewhat impatient. When this is the case, express your impatience in a professional, businesslike manner. While it is obvious to say do it professionally, be careful that there is no anger in your outreach.

When I get impatient, I can appear and sometimes get indignant if I am not careful. So you need to be careful how you word or express your impatience. You have to do it in a way where you can recover from it if the person was just busy versus uninterested. A poor example of impatience (yes, I learned the hard way) would be an email that reads, "Thought I would have heard from you by now? I will assume you are not interested." While the person being uninterested may have been the case, that was not the way to say it. Letting anger come through sort of opens you up for a bitch slap and some loss of credibility. Impatience can also border on appearing desperate or panicked, and people rarely respond to desperation or panic in business. Sometimes I will pen an email, and save it and sleep on it. Almost always, I am glad I did that, and I end up redrafting it to be lighter in tone.

Here's a last word on patience for you. Even if you are losing patience, take a light approach. In the example above, a better outreach would have been: "Hey, I have not heard back from you, and rather than keep bothering you more, I'll check back in thirty days." In this way, you do not look panicked (even though you probably are), and you actually look cool, with other things to keep you busy. This approach may actually draw them back in or have them move quicker.

PERSISTENCE

There is a fine line between persistence and stalking. For me, that line is probably when I keep asking the same question ("Hey, you gonna buy?") over and over again and don't provide any added value or new information. If I can reach out with some value to the prospect/ customer, then I feel better about the multiple contacts. In fact, that is a modus operandi for me—providing value or new information— as it gives me the best chance of engagement. If I cannot provide value or new information, and it is the second or third outreach, that is stalking.

Keeping a diary and/or tracking activities will also provide you with a metric for persistence versus stalking. If you read *The Diary of Year One*, you will see that I was religious about tracking my outreaches and trying to stay persistent without stalking. Imagine yourself in the person's shoes that you are reaching out to (being persistent with!). How does it feel to be on the receiving end of what you sent and what you are about to send? Does it feel good and warranted, or does it feel desperate? It may go without saying, but if you are too persistent, you may look desperate. As I have proffered, in business nobody buys from a desperate seller.

In some cases, you might have to take a longer view and play the long game. If you measure persistence in a fiscal quarter, that is one measure. Alternatively, in some instances, if you measure persistence over a three-year horizon, that is an entirely different measure. In the first measure, you are possibly being too persistent for some situations, while in the other, you are applying the right amount of patience when you have time.

It took me a while to learn this. I came to realize that I was not going to get every prospect to be a client on my timeline and that I was building an enduring business. I was building something to hopefully last for decades (and my first business is, in fact, coming up on eighteen years of being in business and growing). As such, if I needed to back off my persistence and be patient and wait another year or two in certain situations, then I would. Said another way, there were times I had to say to myself: "I cannot close this deal with this prospect or company right now, but I may be able to in a few years, or next year?" While you cannot use this rationale for all your deals (because you would go out of business), you can pick a few for a longer horizon and some patience. When you play the long game, you live to fight another day. You turn "not now" into "when."

PANIC

The famous last scene in the movie *Scarface* comes to mind when I think of real panic. In this scene, Al Pacino comes out of the office of his lavish home after being shot up, with his machine guns blazing, and yells, "Say hello to my little friend!" He lets a grenade launcher blast and then proceeds to get shot to pieces and falls a few stories into his indoor fountain—dead! Call it adrenaline, call it cocaine, call it going out in a blaze of glory—it's also a good example of panic.

Not panicking is easier said than done. But please, please, do not ever show panic. There are times you will panic or be panicked, but do not show others around you. It will erode all the good you have done and want to do. The human condition smells and senses panic, and in business, it will kill you. Panic destroys the ability to choose between patience and persistence and backs you into a corner. As the leader of a new enterprise, you have to sit on panic and deal with it in private.

That said, some panic is coming, so here are some thoughts for you to consider:

Walk away and catch your breath. I am not advocating running out of the room in the middle of a situation, leaving people wondering, "What the heck just happened here?" I am talking about bringing a meeting or situation to a rapid close and leaving the door open for tomorrow. This situation would feel like this: "You know, there is a lot to consider here, and I am going to need a few days" or "I need to speak with some folks and consider this." If or when things get a little crazy, you have to take measured control (of the panic) and quickly close the topic with what is going to happen. I would also advocate that you give yourself days or weeks versus hours or a "by the end of tomorrow" deadline. If truly panicked, you need to buy some time and perspective, and that takes a day or more.

Change your business perspective. You have to know when you are holding the bat too tightly. In the heat of a moment, every-thing may seem like life or death, or deal or no deal. I have found there were times where I created that for myself and did not need to. It is easy to put timelines or an importance on things that might turn out to have been unrealistic. In our quest to move fast and succeed, you may have set up impossible goals (see Law 19, the Law of Twos). When that happens, you can run the risk of panicking about something that did not need a panic! I called that holding the bat too tightly. Why?

A baseball analogy: To hit a baseball well, you need a mixture of a firm but relaxed grip on the bat. If you hold the bat too tightly, tensing everything up, you are unable to hit well. If you hold it too loosely, you are also unable to hit well. It has to be a comfortable mix of firm and loose to hit well. The same holds true in business. There are times where maybe there is a lot riding on something (like a key sale or key milestone), and if you hold it too tightly and ride it too hard, you're bound to mess it up. If you find yourself holding the bat too tightly or getting wound up, take the afternoon off. Take a long walk, catch your breath, and step back to get some perspective on the right/best things to do.

If you are going to panic or act irrationally, make sure it is not a critical issue (big client/prospect, key deal, key hire) and it is self-contained. There are times when *panic* may just take hold and you do something that, the next day, you know was a screwup. You can always tuck your tail between your legs and apologize. If it happens, be honest and quick: explain the situation ("I am not sure what came over me, but I lost it; I am sorry") and see if you can move forward. We are all human, and there is room for forgiveness, depending on the issue.

Another way to manage panic is to use a life-framing perspective. My pivot, when I felt or feel a panic, is to ask myself this fundamental question: "Is my health or the health of my family at stake?" In business, I always found the answer to be *no!* If I do not have my health or my family does not have their health, those are real panic moments. Everything else is, relatively speaking, bullshit! Even if the panic situation meant I was unable to pay some or all bills on time, or miss deadlines, or go bankrupt, it never was going to affect my health or the health of those who mattered. A larger perspective can help to keep things in true perspective.

Here's a last word on panic for you. In the early days of a few of my ventures, I would actually take a good half day or full day and go to the local library to gather my thoughts. Getting away from things and stepping back in a quiet place was good for me (and the business). In fact, I am typing most of this book in a library because when I try to do it at home, I sort of panic because it never seems to get done. The library days gave me time to step back, let go of the bat, and help advance things.

LESSONS LEARNED

Know the situation you are in and especially the time horizon.

I outlined this business model in a prior Lesson Learned or two, but it also applies here in a slightly different context. So although I am retreading some ground, I feel it's worth repeating. This story may be a little complicated, but stick with me.

In 2004, I started a benchmarking business which, simply put, relied on getting five separate pharmaceutical companies to provide me detailed information, about the same things, at the same time. Sort of a tricky business to start in getting five distinct companies to cooperate on something entirely new to them, simultaneously?

About six months into starting the business, I had four clients (not five) signed up. I was struggling to get the fifth. I had three prospective companies considering the fifth slot, but it was going slow. The four companies that had signed on were starting to get impatient to get going. I was in the triangle of emotions, teetering between patience, persistence, and panic. What to do? I took some time and decided I had two choices:

Option 1: Wait for the fifth client to join. I could have waited for the fifth client to join before I did anything. For me, that would have probably caused me to be too persistent with (stalking) the remaining three prospects and maybe end up not getting them. In this situation, I might have created too much self-inflicted pressure, where I would end up panicking and being too persistent with each of them, stalking them for an answer? This may have given me three nos, and I would end up never getting the fifth.

Option 2: Proceed with the four, and give us time (but risk) on getting client 5. For this option, I could take the calculated risk of starting with the four clients we had and being patient with the fifth spot among the three prospects. I could even afford to keep going to new prospects for the fifth spot beyond the three I had. The downside was the potential to never get the fifth and only have done it with four. I looked at that potential outcome as unlikely. I also felt that if that happened, then I really was not going to be in business, and I might as well go out in a blaze of glory.

I chose option 2: start the benchmark work with the four clients I had under contract and work hard to land the fifth. The four clients that started were slow to start anyway, buying me even more time (and patience) than even I thought I had. Starting with the four also created a momentum of being up and running for other prospects to see. In working with the four, we were also able to learn and talk smarter with the potential new clients. Eventually, we not only got the fifth client but ended up getting a sixth, exceeding the goal.

This entire decision is an example of the triangle of emotions. Should I be patient (and wait), persistent and keep pinging the three prospects, or panic by not starting with the four *and* annoying the hell out of the three prospects? On any given day, I was not sure what to do. But with a little time (some sleep, long walks) and perspective, I decided to start with the four and be patient (yet persistent) with the three prospects, *and* I added a goal of getting three additional prospects (versus just relying on the known three) as insurance.

Key takeaway: The point of this sort of long and complex story is that by applying patience at the right time, being persistent when I needed to be, and avoiding panic (at least in my clients' eyes), we made it. While I was surely panicked internally, I never let the panic beast out of the cage, affording me the choices of when to be patient and when to be persistent.

Footnote: I don't feign perfection on the triangle. Many times, very early in my work life, I surely panicked and ruined shit ("Why the hell did Gerard do that?"). There were times I was so persistent about promotions and assignments for my career that I wore out my welcome ("Oh, shit, here comes Gerard again"). And there were times where impatience got the better of me ("Why didn't Gerard wait to do that, like I asked him?"). My experiences with the triangle of emotions have mostly come the hard way—with failures.

Law 16—Resilience and Being Hardheaded: The Difference

Through endurance we conquer.

—Sir Ernest Shackleton

Your ability to celebrate success and recuperate from failure on a daily basis will be an important trait to have and nurture in maintaining your sanity. Additionally, knowing when to pivot or move on will also be important to understand to achieve success. While I am not sure that resilience is teachable, or that hardheadedness is coachable, here are some thoughts to help you navigate these traits. Increasing your resilience can happen when the following occurs:

- When the idea/business gains increasing amounts of traction, it will build your confidence and bolster your resilience. From the very early days of the initial idea through its evolution, if you are receiving positive (verifiable) traction, you should gain resilience. I emphasize *verifiable* here, as the positive feedback should be coming from multiple stakeholders like clients, advisors, consultants, and associates on multiple occasions. It is sort of parallel to the one question you do not want to ask in a sales call (Law 10: "Can I send you a proposal?"); the same applies here. If you are getting unsolicited, good feedback, then your resilience should grow. Conversely, if you have to ask for feedback and almost feel like you're soliciting people to say something nice, that is not good.

- You're making sales. Nothing increases confidence and resilience like a client spending money with you. There is a saying that "revenue is the best perfume," which I can't argue with.

- People are willing to recommend you in aggressive ways. If you find that people are reviewing what you are doing and not only are they interested, but they make an unsolicited offer to refer you to someone else, that should serve to add some fuel to your resilience gas tank.

- You start receiving incoming questions and curiosity, versus you always having to reach out. There are times where you might start to see some word of mouth happening, and people will be reaching out to you. Once again, it's resilience fuel.

If you feel your resilience waning at times, that's OK. You are doing something very hard to do, and you need to have the mental and physical fortitude to stay at it. That said, if your resilience is waning and you are not getting good feedback and/or sales, you might have to checkpoint the whole thing and work to decide to pivot or change/adapt what you are doing. That is where the difference between resilience and hardheadedness comes into play.

RESILIENCE VERSUS HARDHEADEDNESS

A lot of what I outlined in Law 15 (the triangle of emotions) also applies here. I cannot stress enough that taking a break for a few hours, or a day, can be a big help in regaining energy for the business. It also helps to get some distance and perspective on the business. In saying that, here is an example of the difference between hardheadedness ("I am not taking a break; I am staying at this until it is done") and resilience ("I need a break and will come back to this tomorrow") are important. Being too hardheaded runs the risk of wearing you out and wearing those out around you. You need a balanced, calm resilience to provide you the energy and perspective to succeed. Resilience carries with it adaptability, while hardheadedness carries with it immovability (not a good trait to have).

This is probably a good time to cover the concept of finding a mentor. Finding a mentor (or two) who can bring some skills and experience to your situation can be helpful. While you might be fortunate enough to find a mentor who is willing to mentor you for free, you may also find you need to make things worth-

> You need a balanced, calm resilience to provide you the energy and perspective to succeed. Resilience carries with it adaptability, while hardheadedness carries with it immovability

while for them. While I was able to find people who had already made their bones, as they say, to mentor me for free, I also spent some money ($5,000–$10,000) for small projects and advice early on in the business. Even though it was compensated work that I paid for, I considered these consultants mentors and people capable of being honest. I also kept in touch with them and occasionally asked their opinions since they had come to know my business.

Here are a few observations on mentors that might help you find the right one. In my experience of using mentors and being mentored, the best mentors exhibit the following:

- **They make the time for you.** This may sound obvious, but when you have to wait days and weeks for a mentor to get back to you, that is not good. Said positively, a true mentor will make time for you at just about any hour of the day ("Hey, call me after dinner tonight" or "Hey, call me in the car in the morning" or "Hey, can we talk over the weekend?").

- **Organize your issues into manageable and prioritized buckets.** You need to treat a mentor's time as very valuable and group your issues into manageable buckets (versus a list of a hundred). You cannot call them many times per day or per week with small questions and be a nuisance. Maybe instead of making it as-needed, you try and schedule time every one to three weeks to catch up. When you are with them, make sure to cover the most important issues first in case you run out of time. I have seen and experienced mentor sessions that spend too much time bemoaning issues and commiserating versus getting answers and thoughts to more relevant and pressing issues.

- **Mentors are fully present when you are with them (versus being busy doing other things when you are together).** A true mentor can remember what you have been challenged with from prior discussions and ties issues together. Said another way, they are really listening and taking your issues on board. They recall what you talked about last time and use it to form the basis of questions they ask and opinions they give.

- **Good mentors ask good questions before providing advice.** They ask insightful questions that, in and of themselves, make you pause, and they ask a lot of them. They want to really assess what you are dealing with before providing thoughts.

- **It's about you, not them!** I cannot tell you how many times I called someone for advice and ended up giving them advice, never really getting to my issues. Mentors realize it is more of a one-way street (you need their help) right now. This can and should change as time progresses, but in the early days, you need the help and the mentor, not vice versa.

- **They bring real-life, relevant, and recent experiences to your discussions.** They can tell stories that have meaning and applicability for you. They can cite successes and failures with great detail that has relevance to your situation. Said another way, be careful that a mentor is not past their prime or has been on the sidelines so long that their experiences are not 100 percent relevant. I have had occasions where I wanted for someone to be a mentor really badly and then came to realize they had lost touch with the business world.

- **Relevant mentors can also refer you to other mentors and people who can provide advice or services (lawyers, accountants, bankers, and so forth).** They are active and respected in the areas you need mentorship.

- **Finally, a good mentor stays in rhythm with your business.** They reach out to you to see how things are going or call you to ask the particular results/outcomes on something they provided advice on. I have used the analogy of jogging. For me, to be a good mentor, I need to "jog" next to your business and stay in rhythm with it. Said differently, if I find myself retreading old stories or asking again what the situation is/was, then I may in fact be a drag as a mentor versus a help. Good mentors are interested enough in the business and challenges that they jog alongside the business, versus starting and stopping.

A word of caution: Do not expect mentors to help you get business. Finding good mentors is different than networking for sales leads and referrals. While a mentor may reach out in that manner and help you, it should not be expected. If you have good stuff, there is a high likelihood a mentor will try to help you get a client or two because they believe in what you are doing. That will take time. In some of my experiences, I have had people reach out to me for advice and supposed mentorship, and their third question was: "Can you help me sell this?" or "Do you know anyone that would buy this?" What a crappy way to act. You came forward like you wanted advice and support, and then turned it into what you really wanted—sales! I turn those types of people off very quickly and offer limited mentorship.

LESSONS LEARNED

Resilience versus Being Hardheaded ... Knowing When to Pivot or Give Up on Something

As I have recounted, I went to work for an early internet pioneer called DrKoop.com. It was not long before arriving there that the famed internet crash of 2000 happened, and things went downhill quickly.

When DrKoop.com started to sink (or get violently ill), I stayed at it, making sales calls and trying to craft good offerings for clients. I was resilient, even in the face of being laughed at in some settings. There was a stretch of roughly ninety days where I felt that I certainly owed my new employer my resilience and wanted to tough my way through the storm. Heck, I knew things would be a challenge and knew we were pioneering something new and that it would take time. Resilience was called for!

After about ninety days, though, I started to hit a rough patch of happenings that I had never encountered before in my career or in an entrepreneurial environment. The ill winds were a series of the following:

I could not get any new sales meetings ... any. It seemed like potential pharmaceutical clients would not even let us/me in the door! It was though we had a virus, and they could see us coughing in the lobby.

I was getting marginal cooperation from employees. I sensed and observed just about everyone was working on getting off the sinking ship. Associates started openly talking about job opportunities and their plans to leave.

Meetings, whether internal or external, were turned into a sort of mockery or "death watch," sharing the latest headlines of our troubles.

Finally, outside investors, who had invested millions, started to be insulting and almost threatening in meetings.

Things were bad.

Key takeaway: During this stretch of my career is where I learned that hardheadedness will get you "killed" if you are not careful. While the initial patches of rough seas warranted resilience, there is a time where you need to move on … and not be hardheaded. I decided that resilience was no longer called for or warranted, and I needed to move on. I left the business that summer after only six months of being with them. They went out of business soon thereafter, for all intents and purposes.

Law 17—Don't Try to Fake Things: People Know!

Real success is not an outward show
but more an inward feeling.

When you need help, just ask for it. While you may feel embarrassed, there is no need to fake things and posture a sense of success if things are tough or you are in a rough patch. People, good people, under stand that starting a business is hard and are normally willing to lend a hand. Conversely, if you pound your chest and posture that things are great when they are not, you are not helping yourself or your business. Not only will people probably sense that things are not going well, but they will not feel prone to help you, and may in fact write you off a bit for posturing. Simply put, nobody likes a faker. This law is not about faking things to the extent you or someone is lying or being untrustworthy. This law is about knowing that asking for help when you need it is OK.

> Simply put, nobody likes a faker.

Below are some BS detectors I have seen in my journey when I knew a business was not doing well and in need of help, but the leader was unwilling to speak truth. If you are struggling and you are saying these, you may be a tad guilty of faking it. If you are doing some of these things, then you risk not making progress and getting help from the people you need help from. This is no time for posing and posturing because by faking things, you are shooting yourself and your business in the foot and actually repelling any help you need:

- "Things are going amazing." Well, if they are, then you clearly do not need other's help.

- "The business is getting great traction." The word *traction* is the code word here for me. When I hear this statement, I usually follow up by asking, "How many sales have you made in the last thirty days?" to try and get a sense of facts versus "traction."

- "We're looking for investors." The word *looking* is the tip-off for me. While some/many business need outside capital, "looking for investors" is a nonserious term for a serious endeavor. If you want me to consider investing, just ask.

- "We just leased class-A office space." You should probably be working out of a garage, kitchen, the local library, or a basement, not spending money on offices. Once again, this intimates you are doing well and don't need help.

- "I've got more business than I can handle." Clearly, no need for help is required! Do you actually have the business and/or do you anticipate it happening?

- "I was always planning to start this business." I sometimes hear this from people who I know were laid off (like I was in 2003). The truth is that most people would have probably worked for their company for much longer had they not been laid off. See the Lessons Learned below.

On the flip side, when you find yourself really needing some help and relying on someone, it's OK to say the following:

- "I could really use your help on *X*." There should be many people you know who would respond to this and actually help you. Remember, it cannot be begging or be desperate, and you should try to be very specific.

- "If you could do this, it would help me get over the hump." There is nothing wrong with laying yourself bare when you need a break.

- "Tell me what I can do to get you on board—I really want you in." In the early days, I cut a lot of deals that were of little to no risk for early clients. I asked for help, but they got an ROI, or at least a good guarantee of satisfaction.

- "I'd owe you big-time if you are able to *X*." There is nothing wrong with the "I owe you one" if you are dealing with the kind of person this resonates with.

A last few words on not faking it: I genuinely feel that people know when others are faking things. There are little tells, as they say in playing poker, where the person signals something. Whether it is in how they say things or using certain code words (like the examples above), or in their body language, or lastly in the physical evidence. Faking success or good times when they do not exist is just BS and a waste of time. Swallow your pride, be truthful in how things are, and ask for help. Everyone wins when you do that. Nobody wins when you fake it.

LESSONS LEARNED

Getting Fired: The Real Reason behind My First Start-Up

After an almost-flawless twenty-year run climbing the corporate ladder in some large global companies, I got fired from a job in October of 2003. *Fired!*

While my firing was part of a downsizing for a company not doing well, a decision was made that I was not needed. I was let go with six months' severance. Until that day, I was typically the one doing the firing. Now the shoe was on the other foot, and I was literally on the sidewalk with the box of belongings from my office in hand.

Some context: After having spent seventeen or so years with large, well-respected global companies, I embarked on an internet sojourn to make my fortune. I had gone from big-company stability to start-up mania. The job I was fired from in 2003 was my third company/job in three years. When I got fired, I could not imagine going on another job interview and explaining why I was out of work and had been with three different companies in three years. It was that simple, really, for me. I could not stand the idea of updating my CV again, going on interviews, meeting with recruiters, and doing the whole get-a-job song and dance. Maybe it was my ego, or maybe it was the times I had interviewed people who'd had three jobs in three years, and I wrote them off. Whatever the reason, I decided at that moment I had to do something different.

Luckily, I was holding a few aces up my (unemployed) sleeve:

I had ideas! I was nurturing three particular business ideas that I felt were good and uniquely suited to me and my skills. I had not taken any action on them, but I did have them formed in my head.

My network was very strong. I had built a focused career in the pharmaceutical industry, which allowed me to meet and know a lot of people. I was fortunate to have a broad reach of colleagues all around the industry, with many of them in executive-level positions.

I had some guts. Although I was coming off three jobs in three years, I got decent recognition (and was also laughed at) for having the guts to chuck my career in large companies and see if I could make my fortune on the internet. Said differently, although on the surface I was failing, people took notice of my guts in what is a fairly conservative industry. I use the word *guts* while others might have used *stupidity*!

I had some—not a lot, but some—money. I was getting six months' full salary and health benefits as my severance package. So I had some runway. Also, I had enough in savings in the bank to give it a try. All that said, I had three kids: twins entering high school and a fifth grader. So college bills were right around the corner—not much room for error.

I had speed and a work ethic. I could move and think fast, and I was never afraid of working very, very hard. I might not be able to outthink everyone, but I knew I could outwork them.

All of these wonderful things being said, let's get back to the point. It took me getting fired to get up the bravery to try and start a business.

Key takeaway: So how does "not faking it" relate to this? In starting the business, if I was to say to people that I had "just decided" to go for it, when most people knew

I was out of work, it would have been fake. I needed to admit to being fired and not fake entrepreneurial bravery. I had sort of been backed into a corner, and if I faked it, everyone would have smelled it on me. I also would have felt like a liar. In that moment of truth, I believe I had people say, "Good for you; can I lend you a hand?" If I had faked it, I think people would have sensed it and quietly said, "You're full of crap, and I'm not going to buy into your story. Best of luck!" Dead on arrival. If you are starting a business, don't be afraid to ask for help!

Law 18—The Golden Moments: This Is Why You Do This!

The satisfaction of being self-made is
the greatest satisfaction of all.

I realize that many of the emotional laws I have covered make this entrepreneurial journey seem daunting and maybe almost impossible. That is not my intent. That said, I guess I remember some of the tougher times more than some of the better times. I also think the laws I have covered get into the grind of being an entrepreneur. Well, this law (Law 18: the Golden Moments), and this one alone, make all the suffering and grind worth it. So if Laws 12–17 have you concerned, this law will hopefully make it all worthwhile. This law is the Super Bowl victory after all the other (law) practice sessions and hard hits you took.

When you close a deal, cash a check, write a check for an employee/partner, get past an obstacle, or have a client thank you for your hard work, you will *glow*. You will walk on air for hours or days and have a feeling of success you have never felt before. These are moments that money cannot buy. They come from sweat and failure and resilience. These are the proverbial home runs in the ninth inning, touchdown passes in the fourth quarter—moments that create an energy that sustains you for long stretches of the journey.

These are the proverbial home runs in the ninth inning, touchdown passes in the fourth quarter—moments that create an energy that sustains you for long stretches of the journey.

For me, the greatest satisfaction, however big or small the dollar amount was, is cashing a check made out to the name of my business. Holding that check was validation you were on the right path. Holding that check showed that someone was willing to trust you and pay you to do something. Holding that check was like passing significant mile markers in a marathon or a race. Holding that check also helped pay some bills.

Here are some moments I would want you to live into so that you can visualize these moments. These are the moments that keep you pressing forward and resilient:

- You have a really good meeting with a prospect where they show real buying signs (or buy!) and also set up the next meetings for you. Your walk from the meeting to your car is like walking on a cloud!

- You get a great referral(s) from someone that helps you open multiple doors and opportunities.

- You nail an idea on how the product/service should look or operate, and it resonates with a lot of people. You bring it to life in a PowerPoint slide, and prospects stop what they are doing when that slide comes up. When you review the product/service, it is like holding your firstborn ... a very proud moment.

- You write a contract or statement of work for a great piece of business. If cashing checks is the pinnacle for me, writing statements of work and contracts is a close second. I also had fun sending bills.

- You hire an employee or consultant who will help advance the business. You also gain some good company to join and bolster you on the journey. You're able to compensate them well. Robert Melillo, Esq., one of my serial entrepreneur friends, recounts the satisfaction he had at a company holiday dinner where he and his partner sat back and, as he put it, "watched our employees enjoy each other's company. Many were people we trained, and some had families with special needs and other issues, and they all came together to appreciate each other's company and enjoy the business's success. I went home that night and realized a business is much more than just generating profits." Cheers to Bob and his recognition of the bigger picture.

- Your company or product/service wins an award. While this could take years, for me, there was nothing better than winning a real award for the business. For me, it was the *Inc.* 500 Fastest Growing Private Companies (five years in a row) and the Philly Fast 100 (four years in a row). Those awards, especially the first *Inc.* 500 award, will always be supreme golden moments for me and all those that joined me in the business.

LESSONS LEARNED

What It Takes to Be Number 1 (Vince Lombardi)

There is a well-known couple-hundred-word article by Vince Lombardi in which he talks about what it takes to be number 1. I keep it by my desk because it conveys a golden moment, well before I started my own business. It basically says that the moment where you succeed is the moment *you put in the time*. It speaks to the rise and grind and the ability to outwork others. My favorite excerpt from the piece is: *And in truth, I've never known a man worth his salt who in the long run, deep down in his heart, didn't appreciate the grind, the discipline.*

For me, this quote helps me vision forward success; when I am grinding away on the work, I can envision the moment when the grind pays off.

As I outlined in story about getting my third client (Procter & Gamble pharmaceuticals), I can tell you exactly where I was standing in the Philadelphia airport when the call came in and I got the good news. I can't drive by that airport or see a P&G product without having an ear-to-ear grin about that moment.

Key takeaway: As you rise and grind, know the golden moments will come!

PHASE V—THE OVER-THE-HUMP PHASE: AT LEAST FOR NOW

Success is merely the process of fulfilling your own hopes and dreams—not the standards set by society, but the standards set by you.

—Barbara Ackerman

The Over-the-Hump Phase comes at about twelve, eighteen, twenty-four, or thirty-six months, depending on the type of business you are starting. This phase signifies you're into what should be a well-formed business that has created services/products that are being purchased on a repeat basis. While you're not ready to declare victory and claim you have figured it out, it feels like you are out of the woods and on your way. It's a feeling.

Even if you are starting a business in which you want to be a solo practitioner and/or a lifestyle business, I believe you will experience all the things I outline in this book. While the goal for some business ventures is to build a large enterprise and keep growing and adding to it, others may want to build something either small or something that fits into their lifestyle. Please don't convey my references to a business's size or scale as the only way to do it. Even if you are geared toward starting a small side hustle in addition to your full-time position, if you launch it, I believe many, if not all, of the phases and laws in this book will apply.

For one of my businesses, this feeling came at about the twenty-four-month mark. We were getting repeat business and continued to get very good reactions to our unique offering. On a more granular level, we had a few things happening at that twenty-four-month mark. Our revenue growth quadrupled between years 1 and 2, going from $175,000 to $775,000. We went from one offering (service) to three offerings. We were successful at penetrating a few tiers (sizes) of customers, so we had different segments to serve and sell to. We had brought on a few employees and contractors who were perfect fits for the business. We were building our processes and methods so that we could scale the business efficiently. It was getting easier to repeat our work. And most importantly, this early on, we confirmed we were the only firm doing a) what we did, b) in the manner we did it, and c) whom we did it for. Knowing we really were unique provided us the proverbial blue ocean to swim in and the fuel to push the pedal to the floor!

Don't get me wrong; we were still nervous about the future, but it probably was an excited nervousness. We had tangible evidence that we were onto something and, therefore, over the hump of starting the business. While we still did not know how far it would take us, or how large it would be, we knew we were rolling. (Side note: We grew the business to just under $10 million in revenue in six years, and just under $18 million in ten years.)

This phase is not necessarily about scaling the business, although you will have to build some processes and systems to grow. This last phase is really about going faster and being more efficient with what you have, and bringing on board what you absolutely need to accelerate.

So you are over the hump—what to do now? Let's jump in!

Law 19—The Law of Twos: Try and Ignore It, but It's Going to Happen

Every adversity, every failure, and every heartache carries with it the seeds of an equivalent or greater benefit.

I included this law in the Over-the-Hump Phase because as you achieve some success, there is a tendency to think it gets easier or faster, especially as you try and introduce new things. As with all the laws, this is not meant to discourage you, but in fact inform you.

The Law of Twos is a *harsh law*. And try as I may, I have never found a way to avoid it, especially when initiating new things. This law is like gravity! You might think you can change it, or even manage it, but gravity always wins. To this day, I continue to experience this law. Whether in the benchmark business I started, the global surf and sunglass business I am an owner in, or other businesses I have invested in or help advise or start, the Law of Twos never failed to reprove itself.

The Law of Twos, or temporarily forgetting it, is caused by optimism, and that is good in a way. You're optimistic that things will move quickly and have relatively few roadblocks. That is not to imply you're pie-eyed and not dealing with the realities and struggles ahead, but more to identify that your probably being a little too optimistic with respect to what it takes to get new things done or launched in the market. It is human nature to be more optimistic, but be forewarned about the realities and the Law of Twos that await you. You are over the hump, as we have said, but the trajectory for growth and for success is not always linear!

Here are the four components of the law:

1. Everything takes about *twice as long* to happen versus your

original plan.

2. Everything comes in *half as large* as you thought it was going to be.

3. You'll need *twice as much* money to get it off the ground.

4. It will take *two times the effort* to get it off the ground, and you'll be working weekends.

Now, while this law, in my opinion, is unavoidable, it should not scare you or mean you should not forge ahead and keep building the business. The key to this law is to recognize it is a possibility and do some planning around it. Let's jump to the actions before describing the law and outline how you might want to think about it.

- Develop one or two financial models that factor the law in, and see what that looks like. Can you survive the Law of Twos? Take your revenue projections for year one, and stretch them out so it takes two years? Take your expense projections and double them in the first year? Take the amount of time it was going to take and double it?

- Examine whether you have the resources and ability to see it through. If you needed more money, where would it come from? If you had to wait to spend certain amounts of money (e.g., office space, new hires, et cetera), what would it mean?

- Use the Law of Twos as a continuous forecasting mechanism and as a way of reviewing optimistic and pessimistic scenarios. Just because you put together a pessimistic (or worst-case) scenario does not mean you lack confidence in the business. It means you want to review what worst-case looks like so you can digest it and avoid it.

Let's take a look at each of the law's four components:

1. EVERYTHING TAKES ABOUT TWICE AS LONG TO HAPPEN VERSUS YOUR ORIGINAL PLAN

When you are doing something new, it's human nature to use the most optimistic timeline and set sail toward that goal. I understand that and encourage it. What ends up happening, though, is almost always quite different. If a goal or series of tasks involve developing a new idea, or getting your first few sales, or just about anything that involves something new, it takes twice as long to happen.

To simplify and repeat something I wrote earlier in the book: The world was not sitting idly by waiting for you to start your business. They were just fine before you started the business. As such, they will not be moving at the speed you are moving or at the speed you want them to move to adopt your first offering or your next one. New stuff takes time.

In my benchmarking business, we thought we could get our first five clients signed in the first six months of the business ... and it actually took ten months. While it was not literally twice as long, you get the point—it takes more time than you think. When we set out to develop new services, which was something we almost totally controlled inside the business, we found it took twice as much time to get the new offering completed.

2. EVERYTHING COMES IN HALF AS LARGE AS YOU THOUGHT IT WAS GOING TO

This part of the law solely applies to revenue and contracts, not expenses. Expenses will come in twice as much (see next description). When you set out to price *new* solutions and services, you invariably put a too high a price and market value on them. The problem is that the marketplace has already placed a value on the types of things you do, so there is a price expectation already set, in a way. Even if you have something premium, the market has gotten used to paying a certain amount for things. Something *new* takes time to achieve its true price or value in the market.

> Something *new* takes time to achieve its true price or value in the market.

Additionally, the market is probably going to demand (want) some type of pricing concession if they are some of the first to buy your product or service. And frankly, unless you have a large trust fund, you are probably going to be creative (or discount) your pricing for those first clients anyway because you want to get traction and momentum with clients onboard.

For my first clients, I had a goal that each of them would pay $35,000 for the service (benchmark), but did offer some incentives (discounts) for being an early adopter. In fact, they came in at:

- Client 1: $17,500

- Client 2: $25,000

- Client 3: $25,000 (and we did the service twice for them)

- Client 4: $25,000

- Client 5: $30,000

We expected $175,000 in total revenue from these five clients (5 x $35,000) and actually received $122,500. We took in about 70 percent of the goal, and while not dead on the rule of 50 percent, it was close. The summary of this aspect of the law is to plan for less revenue than you might expect because new things rarely price at the level they eventually achieve.

3. YOU'LL NEED TWICE AS MUCH MONEY TO GET IT OFF THE GROUND

This part of the law is really a function of the two prior components of the law (twice as long and half as large). It does not take a mathematician to understand that when those two realities collide, you have some cash flow issues. This aspect of the law is worth spending some time on.

- I have extolled the virtue of being frugal with your money. Keep your spending as lean as possible. I did that by not taking any office space in the first two-plus years. As you may recall, I bartered for my first office (desk) in an existing office. My first employees were either hourly or were revenue-sharing-based arrangements. On the revenue-sharing arrangements, I found a few out-of-work, in-between-job executives who believed in what I was doing and were willing to try it with me, for no salary. Simply put, with each of these folks, we negotiated a deal that shared revenue. For every $1 of revenue (cashed checks) I took in, they would get a certain percentage of it. If we succeeded, they succeeded. Two of them eventually joined me just full time because we did so well. This approach helped me manage the need for money in this law.

- If you are raising or borrowing money, raise or borrow more than you think you need. Also, set expectations that you can come back for more. I will not elaborate, as there are books, degrees, venture capital, debt providers, and private equity firms that deal with this all the time. My only point will be to emphasize that you will probably need more money than you expect. If you are able to, finance yourself (see below).

- Finance yourself. A word about lines of credit: While, for me, it was not in the first year of business, I did seek out a very good line of credit from Citibank. While I had to personally guarantee it, it had a lien against my accounts receivable and was then backstopped personally. That allowed me the borrowing capacity and cash flow to spend a little on-the-come, when I needed more money to grow the business. At its peak, in maybe year 4, I had a $1.9 million LOC out with Citibank but had the business coming in to cover it and more ideas designed to grow even faster.

- You may be able to get paid from clients a little quicker for added consideration. While not ideal, you can offer some discounts or added services to clients to make sure they pay you in a timely manner. For me, in my first business, this was not too much of an issue because I was dealing with the pharmaceutical industry, and they pay on time. In another business I am an owner in (surf equipment and sunglasses), that is not so much the case, and managing cash flow is an art form. In that business, though, we have a line of credit that has liens on the accounts receivable and the inventory, hence giving us some cash flow flex. The point here is that managing the cash you have or are owed is very important when developing new things to grow the business.

- I have not, and probably would not have, borrowed from relatives to fund my business. I know many cases where that is not the case, and entrepreneurs tap into their friends and family for cash flow and investment. All I can say is that this method of operation and start-up, no matter how compelling the idea, is not for me. If this is an avenue for you, I suggest you reread the emotional laws a few times, as borrowing from family and friends will probably heighten them.

4. IT WILL TAKE TWO TIMES THE EFFORT TO GET IT OFF THE GROUND, AND YOU'LL BE WORKING WEEKENDS

While I am once again being a little cheeky with this component of the law, it is totally true. When you start a business, at least in my experience, it is all-consuming. I have said to people it is like adding another small child to your family. It is always there, always on your mind, and always in need of some or lots of attention. The balance to this is that if you are doing what you love, you really should not mind the seven-day workweek. Additionally, if you are having some success and seeing growth, you probably want to keep diving in to make it go even faster.

During the launch of my first business, my family was comprised of three kids. We had twins (a boy and a girl) in their early teens and a son a few years younger, all very active. It was a busy household between school activities, after-school stuff, sports, friends, and so forth. My wife had been a kindergarten teacher, but was now a stay-at-home mom and the captain of our house! Simply put, our house and life was a busy place.

My life hack for the endless work required to start and run a business was to get up very early on weekends (and weekdays also) at 5:00 a.m. and get three or four solid hours of work done before the house got buzzing. By 9:00 a.m.–ish, I had already gotten a lot done and could be a totally engaged dad and husband. I also brought piles of reading and work to the kids' games and tried to do the work when the kids were not looking for me in the stands. My wife would also give me a nudge and say something like, "He's up at bat" or "She just went in the game." Teamwork! I would also pile up any easy reading for the end of the day when the kids were in bed, and I could read it while relaxing and watching TV.

The lack of time (and attention) probably ended up with my wife getting the least amount of both. That said, she never wavered or busted me about it. First, she was not that kind of person, but maybe equally, I think she saw the momentum and knew what good would come from the success if we were able to grab it. So, like a good teammate, she played her position, and I played mine, and together it worked (and still does today!).

In a twisted way, there is another "lever" to neutralize this law a little, which I call brute force. In the early days of the business, I truly believed that I had such great and dedicated people join me that we did the work of two times our real headcount. If there were four of us, I really felt we were doing the work of six or eight people. We were focused; we worked weekends when needed and stayed on things relentlessly. I think we all knew that this was our shot at building and being part of something special. As you grow, it is hard to keep replicating that over and over. Also, let's face it—working eighty-hour workweeks is only sustainable for a few years (I think!). But all that said, in those early days, brute force gets a lot of things done.

The other part of this law that adds to the twice-as-long and twice-as-hard is that you're probably switched on all the time. Given that, you need to find ways to compartmentalize things and try to not let work bleed into the house, and vice versa. That's easier said than done. To this day, weekdays and weekends have little work difference to me. Even though I am settled and not working full time, I am switched on all the time. Sending emails to colleagues and collaborators on any day, at any time, has no differential for me. It's not that I expect them all to be switched on all the time also, but I am. Going through the entrepreneurial journey as I have has made what day of the week it is (weekday or weekend) meaningless.

If, for some reason, this law does not materialize, and you are able to do things in half the time, or with half the money or effort—amen! I do not think I need to outline how to go faster if you dodge the Law of Twos … you will know how to hit the gas in that instance.

LESSONS LEARNED

I am an owner in a global surfing equipment and sunglass business, with headquarters in a remote part of Western Australia (as if Western Australia were not remote enough). We have had operations all around the world, and an office and warehouse in California, since 2010. We launched our OTIS eyewear brand in the United States in 2015, on the basis of having OTIS in Australia for a number of the preceding years and having had success with it there.

In our planning, we thought we would do a few hundred thousand dollars in our first year and then ramp up to $1 million in our second year (2016), given our experience in Australia and our success with surf equipment in the United States. In reviewing the plans, everything seemed to line up for the success we planned. Although we knew it would not be easy, we felt pretty good about our plans. What I forgot was to apply the Law of Twos and remember that anything "new" takes twice as long to achieve, and you spend twice as much. It took us roughly four years to hit that $1 million goal, and we also spent twice the money, or three times as much, to do it.

Key takeaway: The Law of Twos is not about failing; it is about the right expectations. The world was not sitting around waiting for our sunglasses to show up. Hence the fact that the market moved slower than we anticipated, and we spent more to do it than we planned. When something is new, plan accordingly ... the Law of Twos awaits you.

Law 20—Metrics, Metrics, Metrics: Scaling Takes Measuring

Try to keep metrics on a lot of your key functions.
Facts will keep you grounded and living in reality.
They will also help you make good decisions.

In case you have not picked up on it yet, I have to unashamedly confess to being a numbers geek. As a numbers geek, metrics are my drug! It's in my DNA. Growing up, I was always counting things and wondering about the metrics of small businesses. I have joked with people that I was the little kid in line at the hot dog stand, deconstructing their business model and wondering how many hot dogs and sodas they sold, what their costs were, how many people they served, and how much money they made each day. It's just in me.

So once again, it is no surprise that one of the businesses I started was a metrics (benchmarking) business. If that was not bad enough, I kept detailed metrics *on* the metrics business! When I started the business, and for a few years, I kept metrics on:

- **Sales efforts.** I wanted to see what was working and what was not. We wanted to see how long it took to close a sale from start to finish—the sales funnel-to-closing ratio. Specifically on the sales funnel, I looked at target clients, prospects we could get to, sales meetings, and closing meetings. We looked at all the successes and their pathways and also reviewed all the failures. By measuring these things, we were able to develop simple algorithms that told me how many genuine prospects we needed at any given time to hit our goals.

- **Work hours.** Where were the staff and I spending our time?

We reviewed how long each aspect of a deliverable took us to make sure our pricing was good and we were making a fair margin. It was still early on, and I was not interested so much in the classic utilization rates that consulting firms use (number of hours that are billable over the total hours worked), but more interested in seeing how long things took to do. I also was not going to build a time-and-materials (bill-by-the-hour) business, but I needed to know where the efforts were going.

- **Revenue timeline.** Once a client was closed (committed verbally or in writing to moving forward), how long did it take to get going on the work? This metric gave me an idea of how long it would take to get paid (cash flow) and also to manage the workload on the number of clients happening at any one time. It was our forward estimate of capacity planning.

A word on revenue metrics: Be careful of putting too much into revenue metrics, as they are the rearview mirror of your business. The revenue you have achieved is important especially for cash flow, but signifies *past* efforts and is not a predictor of future revenues. Your sales efforts metrics will provide that forward-looking view that I recommend you measure heavily. Look out the front window of the car more than you look in the rear view mirror.

If you're not really using your metrics, but merely recording a bunch

> If you're not really using your metrics, but merely recording a bunch of stuff, you may be busy being busy versus being productive.

of stuff, you may be busy being busy versus being productive. I had an example of this recently playing golf. I was keeping records of all sorts of things (driving distance, number of putts, clubs being used, and so on), and then I found I never went back and even looked at them, never mind using them. It was a pure waste of time, so I stopped. When you actually use (chart/graph) your metrics and do something about what you see, then they are worth recording. If not, bag it and make some sales calls; it is time better spent.

Finally, I consider metrics to be the truth tellers. Metrics can help reinforce what you are doing in a good way and also call BS when you are not following them. Metrics also give the employees of your business something to rally around and reinforce what is important.

LESSONS LEARNED

The Diary of Year One, which I have mentioned a few times and is on my website as a free download, is full of metrics, especially sales metrics. I found that measuring just about every effort provided me a rubric/algorithm, which helped me plan. Those sales metrics helped me understand how many active targets I needed, tracked the prospects (targets that had responded and were in play) I was working on, and how and when they moved through the sales funnel to invariably be closed (yes!) or give me a no. It also helped me to not fall into the trap of sales being measured by closed deals or prospect lists—with nothing in the middle.

These metrics were exactly how I discovered the Law of Twos (Law 19) and are good examples of measuring something and then putting into use. Measuring my sales efforts invariably turned into the Law of Twos "algorithm" that I still use today.

I also measured innovation efforts. As we innovated new products and services, I found that it took roughly five or six new ideas to germinate into two or three new pilot solutions, which invariably became one solution that would be successful. By measuring and using that simple algorithm, I constantly knew how many ideas we needed to be capturing, advancing, and betting on. If you marry that innovation with your revenue-growth goals, you end up with a pretty good metric-driven road map on what you need to be doing *now* to be successful in one, two, or three years.

Key takeaway: I think it was Michael Bloomberg (former mayor of New York and Founder of Bloomberg News) that I heard say something that I believe closes out this law well: "In God we trust, but for everything else, bring me data." Amen!

Law 21—Putting It Back into the Business: Double Down

Don't fear failure … fear regret.

Once you see the business working, your entrepreneurial spirit and confidence will want to keep it going and maybe even accelerate it. As such, you will find yourself putting a lot, if not all, of the money you clear (profits) back into the business. It sort of becomes a multiplier effect of confidence. In the couple of business I have either founded or invested in, we put just about all the money back into the business for the first few years for a number of reasons. Here are a few places to put as much money back into the business as possible.

GROWTH (SALES AND MARKETING)

Driving as much growth as possible during the first few years is paramount if you're trying to build a sizable business. Even if you are trying to build a lifestyle or one-person business, you still need to spend a little here. Whether this involves hiring more sales-facing people or doing smart marketing, driving growth is king. There is no better business cologne/perfume than revenue and revenue growth. When you have revenue, you are in the catbird seat to do just about everything else you need or want to do. When you do not have revenue and growth, it infects every other choice you can or want to make.

A word of caution on marketing: I used the term smart marketing (above) for a reason. When the money is flowing in, and you are looking to grow the business, there are going to be no shortage of marketing "opportunities." Whether the opportunities involve industry conference/meeting sponsorships, advertising (digital and in trade magazines or publications), or the other myriad of opportunities, this is where you should still be a little cheap. I say this because I believe at the early stages of a company, there are still better ways to spend money on growth than marketing.

INNOVATION (INVENTING MORE THINGS TO SELL)

If you have entrepreneurial chops, you will find this comes naturally. Sometimes it comes so naturally, you have to curb it a bit, but all things being equal, innovating new services/solutions and products will help fuel growth, reputation, and market presence. Spending on innovation can involve bringing in (and paying) some outside experts to help you flesh out ideas. It can involve focus groups of clients to dig into their needs and test new ideas … sort of a client board.

Innovation is not always about something entirely new. Your creativity might typically drift to totally new stuff, as you may get bored with the old/existing stuff. Challenge yourself and your team to think about ways of innovating what you already have. Making what you have, and what sells, even better is a good use of innovation money and time. Beware that shiny new objects are just that: shiny new objects (see Law 19, the Law of Twos). Existing services or products can be advanced and shined up also. In one business I started, we were constantly adding to some existing services in the early days to make them better. We knew we were innovating when a client would say, "Wow, this has come a long way" or "Wow, you have made this even better." When we heard this unsolicited feedback, we were pleased (and did well). Clients also only have so much capacity to keep buying new things, and if you wear out your welcome with too many new things and are not paying attention to the things they already buy, you risk going backward with them.

HIRING/CONSULTING (FINDING THE EARLY DISCIPLES)

Once some money starts flowing in, you should be looking to either hire or bring on new people. New people can come in the form of the frontline people you need (sales, consulting, account people, and so forth) and also in the form of support people.

Let's spend a minute on support people. I have found many entrepreneurs only want to hire salespeople and/or the people who are customer facing; they seem loath to spend money on what some may call back-office support staff (administrative help, analytical staff, tech support, accounting support, and so forth). If this is taken to an extreme, it can hinder and demotivate frontline people from doing their jobs. I disagree with the frontline-only thinking and have found good success in hiring a good number of office-based (support) staff. I have found that the right support staff makes the frontline folks jobs more productive and enjoyable, not dragging them too far back into administrative/office tasks that were not a fit for their skills. My second "hire" in the benchmarking business was a stay-at-home mom who liked to work with Microsoft Excel. She ended up doing all the Excel-based tables and work for us so that the we could focus on revenue producing work and being customer facing. My third hire was someone to schedule and coordinate all the benchmark interviews and meetings with clients, which was a labor- and time-intensive process. Once again, the support investment allowed true customer-facing people to stay focused on customers. It was not until our fifth hire that we added more frontline support.

A word on hiring: In the early days, I was fervent about bringing people into the company on what I called a mutual try-and-buy situation. Those folks were typically either currently not working or were solo practitioners (in the gig economy) looking to join us. I almost always did a ninety-day, arm's-length consulting contract with them. I would also have an employment agreement as part of the deal so they knew what the position would pay them if they were hired after the ninety days. After ninety days, if we *mutually* saw a path forward, the offer would kick in. I stress the word *mutual* because it truly was. The ninety-day trial period was meant for both parties to see how they liked working together. This also allowed both of us an easy parting of ways without having to worry about employment agreements if it was not working out. This became pretty impossible to do when I was hiring someone who had a full-time job, as they were not going to leave their employer (and the steady paycheck) for a trial period. That said, I always tried to do it and had really good success with it.

PROTECTION

No, I'm not talking about bodyguards or security systems … I am talking about making sure you protect/safeguard a few key things:

- **Contracts.** Spend the money on a good lawyer to make sure your client contracts are the best they can be. More than likely, your fist few contracts were pretty good, but probably not thoroughly reviewed by counsel and/or as airtight as they should be. In the early phases, you were probably as flexible as you had to be go get business, so you may have cut corners. Having a lawyer review your customer-facing documents is money well spent and will go a long way to protecting you and your company and also have you looking polished. I am not advocating have your lawyer look at every contract you do after that, but one should help with the standard template(s) that you then use.

- **Employment and contractor agreements.** Get a thorough review of the agreements you are using for employees and contractors/consultants. Make sure you are protecting your trade secrets and intellectual property (IP) in your working agreements. Even if your first few agreements were not up to snuff, do not let that stop you from making all the go-forward documents airtight.

- **Intellectual property.** As soon as I had some excess funds, I made sure to get the trademarks I needed on what I felt were unique names, phrases, or anything that I wanted to protect. I also filed for a patent on a very proprietary and unique business process we developed. On the patent, it took years of refinement and dedication to attain it, but it was worth it when we got it.

- **Technology.** Make sure you protect and secure any systems, data, or processes you have, and pay for adequate systems and backup. One of the last things you will probably want to spend money on are things in this area, but they will let you sleep easy at night knowing they are as buttoned up as you can afford. Also, as anyone can attest to, the minute your Wi-Fi or computer is not working, things fall apart. Having and protecting your tech investments are critical!

Finally, here are few things I would *not* to do with your extra revenues:

- Try not to spend money early on for things that don't initially and directly matter, like lavish office space or office furniture. Keep it simple. For me, it was IKEA desks and chairs. Even if your office space or surroundings are sort of ratty, your employees/staff will appreciate your focus on what matters, knowing that "someday," we will be in a nicer office. Of course, if you are in a business that has all, or the bulk of, your clients coming to you, you need to modulate this advice. That said, new clients to your new business will admire a decent but frugal nature to your first office.

- Be careful of doing one-off advertising or conference sponsorships, thinking they will be your breakthrough. One and done is just that: one and done! With regard to any marketing, you have to be able to sustain it over multiple cycles, or you are wasting your money. If you want to do a conference sponsorship or an ad in a trade journal/website, or a paid social media partnership (et cetera), try to negotiate a deal where you do it for a longer stretch of time and get more out of it.

- Travel cheap (look at Law 13 and my $55-a-night motel). If you have worked for larger companies you, like me, probably got into some lavish and sloppy travel habits. Well, now it is your money—so beware. Excessive amounts of travel and/ or staying in nice places come later. You will have time to fly first class and stay at the oceanfront hotel when your business makes it … and you will appreciate it more when you do. I'm not advocating traveling dangerously or staying in bad parts of a city or AirBnBs in a shared house with others or things like that, but more shopping for better deals. Lastly, it can be easy to get excited when you get a sales meeting on the other coast and want to get there quickly …. but try to get a few meetings and reasons to fly places. Be frugal and maximize your travel dollars.

- Acquisitions, partnerships, and joint ventures are a waste of time and money when you are small. You need to focus every ounce of energy you have on growing and finding a defendable bluff for your business, and time on anything larger usually never bears fruit. I cannot tell you how many meetings I did after we had some success with people and companies that wanted to "partner," and it turned out they really just wanted to partner with us on our clients, or they were proposing some kind of joint venture that would have been either hugely distracting or marginally good for us.

• Venture capital/investors: If you do not need the money from the outside, then don't waste the time meeting with people to raise money. You can easily rationalize that it will "be a learning experience" or "be good to be on their radar screen" when, in fact, you should be heads-down growing your own business. Believe me, if you grow your business and start becoming known, investors will find you and beat a path to your door.

LESSONS LEARNED

My first "office" was a two-bedroom apartment in Ambler, Pennsylvania, which was a few miles from my house. After two years of being in business (approaching $2 million in revenue) and operating out of my house and the local college libraries, I decided we needed something more permanent. I ended up leasing the apartment for $850 a month on a one-year lease. It was a ratty-feeling walk-up, but was in the center of a sort of cool, small town that was having a renaissance; there were some restaurants and coffee shops where you could get out for a walk. The apartment itself had warped walls (old spackle), radiators for heat, no air-conditioning, and painted (brown), worn-out wood floors. The electric system was from the '50s. It was old.

I had a romantic notion it was great and fell in love with the idea of a different office situation for me and the small tribe we had (four of us, with plans to add a few more imminently). My hope was that there would be a start-up, under-the-radar vibe to the place, sort of like how Apple started in a garage (yeah, right!). It would also be much different than the normal offices we had all grown up in, continuing the vibe of a scrappy start-up. I was right—it was ratty.

On my first day—yes, the very first day of taking ownership of the office (apartment)—I went up the crappy carpeted staircase from the street, and literally, there in front of the locked front door, was a pile of puke and an open (used) condom. I was dumbstruck! Apparently someone had snuck in the night before to be inside, partied a bit and did some other stuff, and left me an opening-day present. I swear this is true; you cannot make this up. My feeling went from one of entrepreneurial pride to a sort of gag reflex. After collecting myself, I proceeded to have a good laugh about this being my first office day and chuckled that it would be something I would remember. I then cleaned it up and got to work.

We stayed in that office for two or three years, and in fact rented the back two-bedroom apartment on the same floor and had ourselves enough space for six to eight folks and two conference rooms. There were days where it was magic (when we had a nice breeze from the outside) and days where we were like, "What the hell are we doing here?" In retrospect, I would have done *none* of it differently. The people we attracted to work for us would quickly get the vibe we were going for, and those who did not understand the shitty offices did not belong in our tribe.

Key takeaway: Invest back in the business every chance you get, but spend that money wisely. When you get the chance to spend money on the finer things a little more lavishly, you will appreciate it even more.

SOME THOUGHTS ON BEING A MIDCAREER ENTREPRENEUR

Entrepreneurship versus Intrapreneurship: Noting the Difference

If you are midcareer and have run things (divisions, projects, and so forth) in larger companies, like I have in my career, and feel they will serve you well in trying your hand at being a true entrepreneur—you are half right. While these skills and experiences will serve you well, they are quite different than the skills needed to be a true entrepreneur.

One of the rages of the 1980s and 1990s was the term *intrapreneurship*. This term was meant to push professionals in larger companies, who were possibly working on smaller/nimbler things, to act like an entrepre-

> Being intra-preneurial is not the same thing as being an entrepreneur.

neur, but within a larger company (hence the turn of phrase *intra*). While I truly think this was a noble spin on things, and I was surely guilty of fashioning my own efforts along those "intra" lines, it does not translate to being an actual entrepreneur. I have met, and continue to meet, people who will tout their running of things in larger companies and try to equate that to being "just like an entrepreneur." I'm sorry, but that's bullshit! Being intrapreneurial is not the same thing as being an entrepreneur. Allow me to expand on this.

If you lead a group, division, area, or region within a larger company, those are wonderful skills to have accumulated. These skills will serve you well if you decide to start your own business. That said, they are not true entrepreneurial skills/talents. Don't get me wrong; these experiences are very strong, but they are not start-up experiences.

I only mention this to give those intrapreneurs a sense of what is to come if they venture out on their own, and to not get too cocky from their corporate résumés. Once you get on the outside, nobody cares about your windowed, corner office with wood furniture and bookcases!

Here are some tangible differences between the two:

	Entrepreneur	Intrapreneur
Paycheck	Zero	You are safe!
Health benefits	How do you even get them?	You are safe!
Pension/401(k)	Zero	You are safe!
Transparency	Everyone sees and knows	You can spin what you want to
Risks	Enormous	Minimal
Rewards	Enormous	Modest (ya get promoted)
Workweek	24 x 7 x 365 (really)	12 x 5 x 250-ish days
Mindset	Engulfs you	Occupies you
Disruption to Life	Total	Contained
Bureaucracy	None	Always some ... lots?
Processes	Invent them	Adapt them ... abide by them?
Excuses	None	Some
Infrastructure	None	Some-a lot

Corporate success will be a big help in starting a business from scratch, but it will not be a guaranteed determinant of entrepreneurial success.

Why Midcareer Is a Great Time to Become an Entrepreneur

I won't belabor the fact that there are very few early twentysomething entrepreneurs like Zuckerberg, Gates, and Bezos ... I hope you know that. And I won't totally discourage you if you want to start a business right out of university. That said, if you are going to start a business (especially a professional services business like a marketing agency, accounting firm, consulting business, legal firm, engineering and architecture, and so forth) or a business that takes a lot of know-how, you may want to wait until you are in your midcareer (general age range of late thirties to early fifties). If you have spent considerable time in the area you are seeking to start a business, then you have probably done what I outline below.

LEARN, THEN LEAD, THEN LEVERAGE: LEARN IN YOUR TWENTIES, THEN LEAD IN YOUR THIRTIES, THEN LEVERAGE BOTH IN YOUR FORTIES

Learn in your twenties. Learn everything you can about the business or role that excites you when you are in your twenties. This is your chance to become an expert in everything about the market, the customers, the competition, the technology, and the industry you seem to be drawn to when you are young. Dive in with both feet. Work late, work weekends, and take on the tough assignments. Ask to join teams working on important projects. This will do two things for you: first, it will help validate that you really liked this area/profession/market space or invalidate it, and second, it will set you up for the next stage (leading).

Lead when you are in your thirties (or sooner). Now that you have learned and become an expert in your twenties, you're ready to learn how to be a leader. Being a leader takes time and experience and is a very important skill set for your career and your potential entrepreneurial ventures. You need to learn how to lead diverse groups of people (employees, contractors, bosses, executives, clients, et cetera) toward goals. While you certainly do not need to wait until you are thirty years old to be a leader, it will take a few years of learning before you are chosen or ready to lead.

Leverage both the learning and leading aspects of your career to start a business (in your forties or earlier). I refer to this as midcareer. At this point, you are ready to take everything you have learned over many years—you've seen numerous economic periods and market cycles—and combine that with your well-honed leadership skills.

By your midcareer you will also have hopefully developed a good network of peers in other companies and established yourself in your industry and market. While this will probably not take you until you are literally forty years old, I would proffer that if you venture out before your early to midthirties, you may not have the best network you would want to have in launching a business.

The point of this cautionary advice is that waiting to being midcareer is OK and maybe even preferred when starting a business. If you have followed the rubric above, whether intentionally or unintentionally, you are probably ready.

EPILOGUE

I can only hope you found the book a good read. As I have outlined, I have tried to make it punchy and fill it with the stories and lessons I have learned with the hopes of bringing the phases and laws alive. I also feel *The Diary of Year One* makes a good side-by-side read, as it also gives voice to this book, and you will see how many laws came into being. You can find a complimentary copy of *The Diary of Year One* on my website (www.stephenegerard.com).

If you are able to take away a few lessons that help you start your business and run and grow it in a more knowledgeable manner than I, I'll be happy. As a lifelong geek and student of business, I know I found great service in books and articles that spoke to me and caused me to be better. Being a lifelong learner, I also took inspiration out of others' stories, and they provided me fuel and energy to get back at it.

I can only hope this book serves to help you advance your mojo for being in business and inventing new things. As a friend once told me:

If you go into business and are fortunate enough to have some success, your life changes forever ... and for the better.

Those words have been so true. Once I started my own business after years of climbing the corporate ladder (and enjoying the climb), everything changed. From the hard first few years to the successful years that followed, it all changed and got better.

I have had the great fortune of working with some wonderfully smart, hardworking people, and they know who they are. I have acknowledged a few of them in the Acknowledgments section that follows. Together we dreamed, risked, built, laughed, worried, stumbled, and thrived on the challenges of being in charge of our own destinies. There is nothing like taking full charge of your future and making it happen. *Go for it!*

ABOUT THE AUTHOR

Rather than bore you up front with a lot about me, I decided to put this section in the back in case you wanted to understand more about my career and credentials.

I started a business after being in the work world almost twenty years. While I always nurtured ideas, had a few side-hustle starts and stops, and had a file in my home desk drawer labeled Start Your Own Business, I did not go for it until I was forty years old and unemployed!

Let me provide some context. At the time I started my first business (late 2003), I had a five-thousand-square-foot house with a healthy mortgage, a stay-at-home spouse, twins in high school (with college around the corner), and another child in fifth grade. Let's just say there was a healthy amount of responsibility (financial, family, spiritual, and emotional) on our shoulders.

I went for it because I was downsized (fired!) from a struggling company that cut out a layer of management to survive. It took getting fired and having some savings and a severance package to actually go for it. I would probably call this "forced bravery"! Even though I had a sizable monthly cash burn in my life, now was the time to give it a go. If I had not been fired, I am not sure I would have ever made the entrepreneurial leap.

While I was always what they called intrapreneurial (which I covered earlier in the book), I was not an entrepreneur until I had twenty years of business experience under my belt. As such, I had a modest idea of better ways to do things, having learned from some of the finest companies in the world: Pepsi Cola, Schering Plough Pharmaceuticals (now Merck Pharmaceuticals), IMS Health (now IQVIA), and SimStar Internet Solutions (now part of the Publicis Groupe). I also got a sense of what types of things and methods I did not want to employ, from observing some poor practices in some of those same companies as well as other companies I came in contact with.

Here's my twenty years of work experience in a paragraph. I came up the ranks (1984–1990) through accounting and finance, so I had a good discipline and foundation in numbers. This is/was particularly useful in doing projections, pricing, and managing the day-to-day operations of businesses. I moved into sales and marketing areas (1990–2003) and had the ability to apply my analytical skills in areas that were more art than science. As I moved up the proverbial corporate ladder, I was provided the opportunity to manage all sorts of great (and some not-so-great) employees in disciplines like technology, consulting, sales, marketing, and service. Being able to lead and manage these varied skills and personality types enabled me to round out my career in general management-type roles. All in all, it was a perfect twenty-year-ride in corporate America.

It was only after being in the business world for almost twenty years and being downsized (fired!) in 2003 that I was really able to contemplate becoming a real entrepreneur. Faced with having been employed by three different internet-based companies from 2000 to

2003 (the early days of internet 1.0) and out of work, I could not contemplate the idea of going on more interviews and explaining the twists and turns and stumbles of the past three years. While I considered myself eminently employable, I was coming off three jobs in three years—so I did not look that employable.

So I decided that "now" (late 2003) was my time to try something. Fortunately I had kept a folder in my desk drawer at home labeled Start Your Own Business, in which I was compiling ideas should the day (and guts) ever come to start my own business. It was in that folder that the idea for TGaS Advisors was born (more on that in a moment). Scribbled on a torn piece of paper was "How do other pharmaceutical companies do it?" with some scribble about finding a "way" to answer this question for pharmaceutical companies.

TGaS Advisors was a benchmarking business in the beginning. In a nutshell, pharmaceutical companies were looking for ways to learn from other pharmaceutical companies, in a collaborative way versus a competitive way. While there would always be things that were "secret" in companies, there had to be a way to gain collective wisdom and learnings from other companies and then funnel fact-based information back to the participating companies (members) to help them make decisions.

TGaS Advisors focused on gathering hundreds and hundreds of data points about a pharmaceutical company's operations. We then aggregated that information into a database and provided those facts and insights back to the participating members. It was that simple: gather data, anonymize and normalize it (make it comparable), and then present it back to the participants. TGaS Advisors was a data-driven "arms dealer" selling "weapons" (data and insights) to whomever would participate and play by the rules.

TGaS Advisors, as well as some of my other larger company experiences, were providing services typically based on multiyear memberships/contracts, annual retainers, or projects. Deals and contract sizes could be described in the millions of dollars, with a high degree of complexity. Clients were generally midsize to large ($500 million to $50 billion in annual revenue) pharmaceutical companies, which operate in a very vigorous and mature manner.

TGaS Advisors was organically funded (I funded the business and then used a line of credit to expand it), was always profitable, and grew from an idea in 2003 to a $15 million business by 2012. We never took outside investment and grew it rapidly. We went from having no employees to almost fifty at our peak.

At TGaS Advisors, we experienced the entrepreneurial dream of selling the business to a larger company in late 2010. I remained on for three more years and "retired" in 2013. But then, in 2014 with a group of investors, I bought the company back and have since sold it (again) in August 2018. Now, while I remain a shareholder in the new venture, I am retired from the company. Two bites of the apple, as they like to say! The rough accumulation of selling-buying-reselling the company was $100 million. I give that number to provide a perspective on the scale of the business development activities ... not provide a sense of that being "my" money!

The majority of my experience is in B2B (business-to-business) environments, with modest experience in B2C (business-to-consumer) markets. My business résumé follows:

Large multinational corporations:

- Pepsi Cola Corporation: 1985–1987

- Schering Plough (now Merck Pharmaceuticals): 1987–1994

- IMS Health (now IQIVIA): 1994–2000

Start-up businesses:

- DrKoop.com: 2000 (about six months)

- SimStar Internet Solutions (now part of Publicis Groupe): 2000–2003

- EduNeering (now part of KaplanEduNeering): 2003 (about six months)

Entrepreneurial start-up/investor/board of directors/advisor:
- TGaS Advisors: 2004–2018; still an investor

- The Leisure Collective International: 2013–present; board chairman and principal in the ownership group based in Western Australia (offices in California and France)

- SEER Interactive: Advisor

- Entrepreneurial advisor and investor in a number of small companies

Other pertinent items worth a mention:
- *Inc.* 500/5000 Awards (2008, 2009, 2010, 2011, 2012)

- Philly Fast 100 Growth Companies (2008, 2009, 2010, 2011)

- Philadelphia Smart CEO Future 50: Top Growing Companies (2011, 2012)

- CEO Top 50 (2012)

- 100 Most Inspirational People in Pharma Award (2008)

- Patent holder (8606623; https://patents.google.com/patent/US8606623)

- Rider University: BS in finance (1984)

- Certified Public Account: Retired certificate and license (1987)

- Monmouth University: MBA (1989)

- Board of Trustees: Term 2019–2023)

- Most important: Husband (thirty-three years); dad (three adult kids); family man!

Over the last few years, I have become a principal owner in a global surf equipment and sunglass company called The Leisure Collective International (TLCI). I invested in this relatively small ($7M in global revenue) company in 2013 and have become board chair and one of the three principal owners. I do not "run" the business and have a wonderful management team that has doubled the business in the past six years. I'm active with the strategy and important decisions. I recently became full owner of the Americas region and manage that with a team based in California and have my oldest son working in the business.

TLCI invents, manufactures, and distributes roughly two hundred products globally to almost three thousand surf and specialty shops around the world. We operate under the brands Creatures of Leisure (surf products) and OTIS sunglasses. We believe that you can walk into just about any (better) surf shop in the world and find our products on the shelves. We are in the top three of many of our competitive categories. I mention TLCI, as it has also helped shape this book and my experiences.

ACKNOWLEDGMENTS

This book would not be complete without acknowledging a few individuals who have been invaluable business companions in my journey. I'd like to acknowledge those first soldiers of TGaS Advisors:

- Jim Mercante, for being all in from very early on and working so hard

- Candice Baglivo, for her can-do, positive attitude

Both Jim and Candy formed the skeletal and cultural structure for what TGaS Advisors became. Soon thereafter, as we began to add to our army, we added a few more folks in our cramped and dilapidated office in Ambler, Pennsylvania. A big thanks to the folks who made up the "Ambler Eight":

- Mary Ellen Shire, for pioneering many of our processes and her dedication

- Donna Wray, our first full-time salaried person and internet innovator

- Peter Bittinger, for making all our systems hum and automating it all

- Jeff Wojcik, one of our first clients, recommenders, and senior associates

- Kevin Boucher, the perfectionist and tireless analytical mind

I'd also like to thank Martin Driscoll, our first client, day-one reference provider, and two-year team member.

In addition to these folks, I'd also like to acknowledge the following people from whom I have learned valuable entrepreneurial lessons: David Reim and Robert Rebak (SimStar International—my first true small standalone company); John Malloy, Nathan Omodei, and Shane Partington (from The Leisure Collective International); Gary McWalters and John Carro (from TGaS Advisors); Robert Melillo (serial entrepreneur); Len Kanavy, Gerry McKenzie, and David Snow (early clients); David Thompson and Chris Stratton (KP360); Wil Reynolds and Crystal Anderson (SEER Interactive); and Neil Gerard (my brother) and Michael Buckworth (my cousin), who have helped me in innumerable ways and always had my back.

To enhance the book and the Lessons Learned sections, I also drew some of the laws and the stories from colleagues, business partners, and other entrepreneurs whom I respect. I have been fortunate in that my circle of business colleagues is pretty large, and I have had the great fortune of spending time with some world-class entrepreneurs and business thinkers. In writing this book, I reached out to gather their thoughts and stories with the goal of making the book and its stories a little broader and deeper than just my experiences alone. I am grateful to those folks who provided me with their wisdom and experiences.

Finally, I'd like to acknowledge my mom and dad. My dad,

Cornelius F. Gerard was always working on what we would call today his "side hustle." My dad had a part-time insurance business, aside from being a full-time high school teacher. My dad came home every day after teaching all day in a north New Jersey high school and went into his home office and worked another few hours on the insurance business that he inherited from his father, Carmine. That entrepreneurial insurance business helped our middle-class family live a very good life, and with the support of my mom, Doris, they were able to carve out a very good life for our family. My mom was a legal secretary and also did typing at home, after retiring to raise a family. She actually helped a retired judge get his book transcript together. My entrepreneurial genetics go back for generations.